The Complete Guide to Pomeranians

Vanessa Richie

LP Media Inc. Publishing

Text copyright © 2019 by LP Media Inc.

All rights reserved.

No part of this book may be reproduced or transmitted in any form or by any means, electronic or mechanical, including photocopying, recording, or by an information storage and retrieval system - except by a reviewer who may quote brief passages in a review to be printed in a magazine or newspaper - without permission in writing from the publisher. For information address LP Media Inc. Publishing, 3178 253rd Ave. NW, Isanti, MN 55040

www.lpmedia.org

Publication Data

Vanessa Richie

The Complete Guide to Pomeranians ---- First edition.

Summary: "Successfully raising a Pomeranian dog from puppy to old age" --- Provided by publisher.

ISBN: 978-1-08000-5-116

[1. Pomeranians --- Non-Fiction] I. Title.

This book has been written with the published intent to provide accurate and authoritative information in regard to the subject matter included. While every reasonable precaution has been taken in preparation of this book the author and publisher expressly disclaim responsibility for any errors, omissions, or adverse effects arising from the use or application of the information contained inside. The techniques and suggestions are to be used at the reader's discretion and are not to be considered a substitute for professional veterinary care. If you suspect a medical problem with your dog, consult your veterinarian.

Design by Sorin Rădulescu

First paperback edition, 2019

TABLE OF CONTENTS

INTRODUCTION **9**

CHAPTER 1.
Breed History And Characteristics **10**
Descended From Hardworking Dogs 11
A Favorite In Show 15

CHAPTER 2.
Loyal, Mischievous Charmers – Determining If The
Pomeranian Is The Right Breed For You **16**
Descriptions And Defining Characteristics 17
   Appearance 18
Temperament 19
Ideal Environment For Pomeranians 21
Even No Yard Is Fine – As Long As Your Pomeranian Gets
Moderate Exercise 22
A Natural Learner 23

CHAPTER 3.
Finding Your Pomeranian **24**
Puppy Versus Adult 25
   Adopting A Puppy 25
   Rescuing A Pom 27
   Pomeranian Clubs And Rescues 28
Adopting From A Breeder 30
   Health Tests And Certifications 30
   Contracts And Guarantees 30
   Puppy Genetics – The Parents 32
   Finding A Breeder 33
   Selecting Your Puppy 36

CHAPTER 4.
Preparing For Your Puppy 38
Preparing Your Kids 39
    Always Be Gentle 41
    Chase 41
    Mealtime 41
    Paws On The Ground 43
    Valuables Out Of Reach 43
Preparing Your Current Dogs 45
    Set A Schedule 45
    Leaving Your Dogs' Important Toys And Space Alone ... 46
    Getting An Idea How Your Dogs Will React – Extra At Home Play Dates .. 48
Dangerous Foods 50
Hazards To Fix 51
    Indoor Fixes 52
    Outdoor Fixes 55
Supplies And Tools To Purchase And Prepare 56
Choosing Your Vet 57
Planning The First Year's Budget 59

CHAPTER 5.
Bringing Home Your Pomeranian 60
Final Preparations And Planning 61
The Ride Home 63
First Night Frights 63
First Vet Visit 67
The Start Of Training 69

CHAPTER 6.
The First Month 70
Not Up To Full Strength – Don't Overdo It In The First Month 72
Setting The Rules And Sticking To Them 74
Treats And Rewards Vs. Punishments 76
Separation Anxiety 78
Training Areas To Start During The First Month 79

CHAPTER 7.
Housetraining 80
Inside Or Outside – Potty Training Options 81
    Your Housetraining Options And Considerations 82

Setting A Schedule And Outdoor Restroom Location 83
Key Words 84
Positive Reinforcement – Rewarding Good Behavior 84

CHAPTER 8.
Socialization And Experience 86
The Importance Of Socialization 88
Properly Greeting New People 91
Behavior Around Other Dogs 91

CHAPTER 9.
LIVING WITH OTHER DOGS 92
Introducing Your New Puppy 92
Establishing The New Norm 95
Biting, Fighting, And Puppy Anger Management With Multiple Pom Puppies 97

CHAPTER 10.
Training Your Pomeranian Puppy 100
Firm And Consistent 101
Gain Respect Early 101
Operant Conditioning Basics 102
Primary Reinforcements 102
Secondary Reinforcements 103
Why Food Is A Bad Reinforcement Tool 105
Small Steps To Success 106
Basic Behavior Training 106
    Chewing And Nipping 106
    Crate Training 107
    Barking 107
    Why You May Want To Plan To Have A Trainer 108

CHAPTER 11.
Basic Commands 110
Why Size And Personality Make Them Ideal Companions 110
Picking The Right Reward 111
Successful Training 112
Basic Commands 113
    Sit 113
    Down 114
    Stay 114

Come 115
　　Leave It 115
　　Quiet 117
　Where To Go From Here 117

CHAPTER 12.
Nutrition 118
Why A Healthy Diet Is Important 119
Commercial Food 120
Preparing Your Food Naturally At Home 121
Puppy Food Vs. People Food 122
Weight Management 123

CHAPTER 13.
Exercising – So Easy, Yet So Critical 124
Exercise – Essential Need To Stay Active 126
Playtime! 128

CHAPTER 14.
Grooming – Productive Bonding 130
Grooming Tools 131
Managing Your Pomeranian's Coat 132
　Puppy 132
　Adulthood 134
Cleaning Their Eyes And Ears 135
Bath Time 137
Trimming The Nails 137
Brushing Their Teeth 137

CHAPTER 15.
Health Care 138
Fleas And Ticks 139
Worms And Parasites 140
Benefits Of Veterinarians 141
Holistic Alternatives 142
Vaccinating Your Pomeranian 143

CHAPTER 16.
Health Concerns 144
A Dog With A Lot Of Possible Health Concerns 145
　Face 145

Body	145
Typical Purebred Health Issues	147
Where You Can Go Wrong	148
Importance Of Breeder To Ensuring Health In Your Pomeranian	148
Common Diseases And Conditions	149
Prevention & Monitoring	149

CHAPTER 17.
Your Aging Pomeranian

Your Aging Pomeranian	150
Senior Dog Care	151
Nutrition	153
Exercise	153
Mental Stimulation	154
Regular Vet Exams	154
Common Old-Age Aliments	155
Enjoying The Final Years	156
Steps And Ramps	156
Enjoy The Advantages	156
What To Expect	156
Vet Visits	157

INTRODUCTION

The Pomeranian is one of those canine breeds that you can easily identify on sight. They look like stuffed animal versions of lions, which is actually a hint of what their personality is like. Pomeranians have a double coat, which contributes to their lion-like look. That means you will have to make grooming a regular part of your routine. Despite being small dogs, they have a huge personality. They are a vocal breed, and will march right up to much bigger dogs and bark to let them know who is boss.

This is also quite an intelligent breed, so training your Pomeranian will be fairly easy as long as you are firm and consistent. Since they are headstrong, you need to let them know that you are the boss. Once they understand their place in the pack, they are a fantastic addition to the family. They love to play games and perform tricks to keep you entertained.

Although they are a great addition to the family, Pomeranians are not an ideal choice for families with young children. As excitable and energetic as Pomeranians are, this can be a bad combination with young kids who don't understand that they have to be careful when playing with little dogs.

Even though they have a good bit of energy, Pomeranians' small size makes it fairly easy to make sure they get more than enough exercise by playing at home or going for half hour walks a couple of times a day. As Pomeranians are such quick learners, you can both be entertained by continuing with training lessons over the entire life of your pup. They are also a great lapdog because they aren't any bigger than a cat.

Pomeranians are a great breed for most families. They do require training to keep them from being incessant barkers, but it isn't nearly as challenging as it is with many other small breeds. With their fearless appearance and personality, this is a great breed for people who love to travel or stay at home.

CHAPTER 1.
Breed History And Characteristics

"Poms are intelligent, playful little things. They will wander if off their lead, so be careful. They are brave and inquisitive and do not realize how tiny they are."

Claudia Wallen
Pearl Moon Poms

Pomeranians look nothing like their ancestors, starting with their size. To look at the little breed of dog, you would expect it to have originated from other small dogs that were kept as companions. However, the Pomeranian actually looks like a very shrunken version of what it used to be. Their history is really what has made this such a fun-loving and endearing breed.

Photo Courtesy of Rachel Lubbe

CHAPTER 1   Breed History And Characteristics

Photo Courtesy of Kat O'Brien

Descended From Hardworking Dogs

"Because they are descended from a large sled dog breed (Spitz, Husky, Malamute, etc) they have the mentality of a large dog in a small package. Most know no fear."

Gary & Janie Burnette
Burnette's Exclusive Pomeranians

Given how little the Pomeranian is, it is difficult to guess at its ancestry. Today they are the smallest Spitz breed, but like all of the different types of Spitz breed, they can be traced back to 400 BC. Different evolutions of the breed appeared across both Europe and Asia, making it difficult to determine a point of origin for the family. The fact that different regions identified dogs in the family by names based on the language of the region makes it more difficult to pinpoint how the breed evolved to be as diverse as it is today.

Though the family does have roots that extend back a couple of thousand years, the name Spitz did not enter common use until the 15th century. Coming from a canine family with such blurred origins, there is more

CHAPTER 1   Breed History And Characteristics

speculation than fact about the specific origins of the Pomeranian within the family. In France, older versions of the breed were called Chien de Pomeranie or Lulu. However, there were nearly identical breeds in Italy that applied several names to it based on the region of Italy during the 18th century. The Italian breeds of the time displayed the bright orange coat commonly associated with Pomeranians. The earliest attempt to classify the breed was done as part of a larger effort by Carl Linnaeus to classify the different dog breeds. A Swedish naturalist, Linnaeus spent most of the 18th century working to identify and document as many European breeds as he could. His writing of the Canis Pomeranus was not extensive, and largely showed that the breed was fairly widespread across Europe.

> **HELPFUL TIP**
> **American Pomeranian Club**
>
> The American Pomeranian Club is the official American Kennel Club-recognized National Parent Club for this breed. The American Pomeranian Club is a non-profit organization, with all proceeds from its website and events going toward breed-related issues.

Prior to the 15th century, some of the breeds in the family were called Chien-loup, which is believed to have been derived from the French term lou-lou. Today the family is closely associated with Germanic roots, as indicated by the very Germanic family name. When King George III ascended the throne, it is likely that the Germanic name became more widely used, particularly among English speakers. When Queen Charlotte married King George III in 1761, she brought her little "wolf-like dogs" with her to England. Her Pomeranians were largely white, instead of the reddish-orange of the fox. The name Pomeranian comes from the region where the queen's dogs originated, Pomerania in what is now Germany. She was perhaps the first person recorded as calling the breed Pomeranian. Just like today, her dogs attracted a lot of attention, and they often ended up in pictures. They became a more popular breed as people began to imitate the queen across Europe.

About 50 years later, William Taplin more thoroughly documented the breed in "The Sportsman's Cabinet." The term Pomeranian was beginning to replace the term wolf-dog to describe the breed as it became more common. Taplin went in great detail about the appearance of the breed, with the biggest difference being the dog's coat color. Many of the English Pomeranians had white or cream-colored coats, like the queen's. More importantly, he began to discuss how members of this breed should be trained. Despite being a pet to the royal family, Pomeranians were still a working

Photo Courtesy of Melanie Adkins

dog. Many of the methods would be considered animal cruelty today, and did not facilitate the kind of loyalty and trust that training today builds. Over the next 100 years, the breed would be used increasingly less for work and more as a companion.

The breed was growing in popularity, but the Pomeranian did not become a darling of English society until the second half of the 19th century with the advent of dog shows. The second English dog show was held in 1861, and a Pomeranian was given the title of first in class in the category of non-sporting foreign dog. The first Pomeranian Club was established in England during the 1890s, by which time the terms fox-dog and wolf-dog were largely phased out. By this time, more Pomeranians also had the reddish coloring commonly associated with the breed today. Finally, breeders and pet owners were increasingly interested in breeding increasingly smaller versions of the breed. When the 20th century began, the breed was small, but still most of them were at least as tall as their people's knees.

Around this time, Pomeranians began to make their way across the ocean to America as faithful pets. The majority of Poms that reached American shores had been bred in England, so the canine in the US today is more closely related to the English version than the many other Pomeranians across Europe. Just like the original version of the breed entering England were not the color associated with them today, many of the Poms that were brought to the US around the turn of the century were white. Americans were also interested in the Pomeranians that were white, blue, and brown. The National American Kennel Club recognized the breed at the turn of the century. The breed became very popular, very quickly, and by 1900 the American Pomeranian Club began. The club became a member of the National American Kennel Club in 1909.

A Favorite In Show

Queen Victoria was the first to show this amazing little breed. To this day, they remain a constant favorite because of their incredibly unique look. Between 1900 and 1930, they were the most often submitted breed in dog shows. During that 30-year period, the smaller breeds were favored, which is what led to the breeding of the smallest in show. Also, their colors began to change because the more exotic orange was favored.

It was the introduction of the Pomeranian into dog shows that really resulted in the stereotypical breed we have today. The Pom had not undergone many changes until dog shows began. They quickly became a favorite of judges, sparking the interest in focused breeding for color and size.

CHAPTER 2.
Loyal, Mischievous Charmers – Determining If The Pomeranian Is The Right Breed For You

As a part of the Spitz family, Pomeranians display many of the Spitz characteristics, particularly the triangular shape of their ears, the upward curving tail, and their double coat. However, they have evolved over time to have many unique characteristics, including their incredibly small size.

For their size, this breed has a lot of personality, and they do require a firm hand to ensure that they are properly trained. As one of the more intelligent little breeds, they can create a lot of problems if they are not properly trained and socialized. Their small stature may appear to make them a great breed for any home, but the Pom is not a dog that will work for every family.

Photo Courtesy of Kat O'Brien

CHAPTER 2 Loyal, Mischievous Charmers
Determining If The Pomeranian Is The Right Breed For You

Photo Courtesy of
Sherri J Osterland

Descriptions And Defining Characteristics

With a breed as distinctive looking as the Pomeranian, there is little chance that you will mistake any other breed for a Pomeranian, and vice versa. There are several features that make them so distinguished, but it is really the sum of all these aspects that lets you know you have a Pomeranian on your hands.

Appearance

As one of the most popular toy breeds, Pomeranians have a number of physical attributes that make them very easy to spot. The first thing you will probably notice is their diminutive stature. A large, healthy Pomeranian tends to be, at most, seven pounds. Next, you will notice all of that fur that sticks out everywhere. That gorgeous coat coupled with their size makes them easy to mistake for a stuffed animal.

While a lot of people think of Pomeranians as having only orang-ish-white fur, this breed actually comes in an astonishing number of colors:

- Brown, both Beaver and Chocolate
- Black
- Black and tan
- Bluish
- Bluish tan
- Blue Merle
- Chocolate and tan
- Cream and cream sable
- Orange and orange sable
- Red and red sable
- Tri-colored
- White
- Wolf sable

Despite the many different possible color combinations, it is still incredibly easy to spot a Pomeranian. If you aren't entirely certain by l0oking at a dog's stature and coat, check out the pup's face and tail – the last two obvious signs of the breed.

The best way to describe the Pomeranian face is to say it is fox-like. When you shave the Pomeranian's fur, it is much easier to tell just how large those eyes are (the fur tends to make their faces look larger than they actually are). That cute little nose is evenly proportionate to the eyes. And their mouth looks a bit like a Venus fly trap with a pink tongue and teeth. The ears cap it off, making the little breed look more like a toy than an actual animal.

Finally, their tails curl up over their backs in a manner that is almost unreal. When they are happy, that little tail wags all over the place, creating a funny breeze around their fur. At the end of a long day, that excitement can really help you start to destress when you get home.

STORY
Best In Show

As of 2019, one Pomeranian has been named Best in Show at the annual Westminster Kennel Club Dog Show since the title was first awarded in 1907. In 1988, Ch. Great Elms Prince Charming II, owned by Skip Piazza and Olga Baker, and judged by Mrs. Michele Billings, was named Best In Show.

CHAPTER 2   Loyal, Mischievous Charmers
Determining If The Pomeranian Is The Right Breed For You

Temperament

A well-trained and socialized Pomeranian is a great addition to nearly any family. They are extremely enthusiastic and fairly intelligent. If you want to train them to do different tricks, your Pomeranian will likely adore the extra attention.

For such small dogs, they have a lot of energy. They also have absolutely no fear – your Pomeranian will very likely march right up to any big dog you encounter and act like they are the same size. This apparent lack of understanding of their relative size makes them exceptionally endearing. However, that lack of fear can also cause some problems.

Pomeranians can be a bit territorial, leading them to think they need to stand up to other dogs to protect their people. This can be problematic when they approach strangers. Socialization can help teach them that strangers and other dogs are all right, but there may always remain a bit of suspicion during initial greetings. However, once your pooch gets accustomed to any other pets in your home, your Pomeranian will get along with them just fine.

They are also a fairly intelligent breed, making them great companions if you want a dog that does tricks. They have a lot of energy too. Obviously really long hikes are out of the question, but you can go out for a long stroll or have a long play session.

One of the things you do need to be aware of before picking up your Pomeranian is that this is a breed that is quite vocal. They make a great watchdog because of their barking. However, you are going to need to plan to spend some time training your Pomeranian not to bark all the time. They are notorious barkers without proper training.

These pint-size pooches just don't understand what fear is, which makes them incredibly entertaining and charming. Despite their diminutive size, you aren't likely to find anyone putting a Pomeranian in a bag and carrying them around like some other toy breeds (it's not good for any breed anyway). This is because they don't really inspire you to feel overprotective of them. They know how to handle themselves and they are much happier walking beside you. And you definitely want to make sure it stays that way. Over-pampered Pomeranians can be exceedingly difficult to manage.

Give your Pomeranian the space to be an individual and enjoy your little friend as a companion. It is likely they will stay close to you most of the time because they love their pack.

Photo Courtesy of Debbie Deardorf

    The confidence they exude does mean you have to be firm with them. Housetraining can be a real challenge if you have a particularly headstrong Pomeranian. That and their barking are two of the biggest issues that people face. These are part of the breed's personality, so if you plan ahead, you can avoid most of the problems that some people report having with the breed.

A part of work dog genetics is a stubbornness that can be incredibly annoying in the early days. Be aware that you are going to need to be very firm and patient with your Pom. It will be more difficult to train an adult Pomeranian, but you need to be just as firm and patient with them. Depending on their history, they may not be as difficult as a puppy because they will understand more quickly. Puppies typically do take longer to train, but you won't have to deal with any undesirable behavior that is ingrained. Regardless of your Pomeranian's age, do be prepared for some pushback. It isn't anything they have against you, they just have a strong will and need to be trained to respect you. This is best learned through firm, consistent training.

Your Pomeranian will probably want to sleep in the same room with you (though sleeping on your bed may not be the best idea given their size). This may or may not be all right, depending on if they see themselves as being in charge. Stubborn streaks can be difficult to work through as you have to keep a level head without losing your temper. As long as you keep the rules the same and don't make exceptions, you should be able to help stave off the worst of the stubbornness inherent with the breed.

Ideal Environment For Pomeranians

Pomeranians can fit comfortably into nearly kind of home, large or small. Their diminutive size makes them perfect for apartments (as long as you train them not to bark excessively). Their vivacious nature makes them able to easily get around much larger homes. Because of their size, when this breed gets frisky, they will almost certainly have more than enough space for play without you worrying about them getting hurt.

They are also not a great breed for families with small children. It is easy to hurt a Pomeranian because of their small stature, and small children don't understand when you try to explain about being gentle. If you have a young child and really want a Pomeranian, plan to wait a few years until your child is old enough to understand to be careful before bringing your puppy home. Despite their bravado, Poms are quite fragile, so for the sake of your children and your Pom, it will be best to wait until your child understands how to be gentle.

Even No Yard Is Fine – As Long As Your Pomeranian Gets Moderate Exercise

If you were to get one of their ancestral breeds, you would have your work cut out for you trying to keep a Pom from being overexcited and rambunctious at home. Pomeranians may have a lot more energy than most other toy breeds, but they have very short legs, making it easy to tire them

Photo Courtesy of Penny Hall

out without taking incredibly long walks. A couple of 30-minute walks or a lot of indoor play will be more than enough to burn a lot of that energy. Once they have gotten familiar with an area, they will be more than happy to bounce around you, keeping you in sight and entertained. With that herding element in their genetics, they will be happiest when everyone is together. The bigger the home, the more energy this kind of activity could expend.

Since they are such a small dog, you should not leave your Pomeranian alone outside. Birds of prey can easily carry them away from your home. For your dog's safety, make sure you don't put them outside alone. It is best to keep your Pom on a leash when you go outside. As we will discuss later, this is actually an ideal way of housetraining them as well.

A Natural Learner

Pomeranians have spent several hundred years as companions to humans, and much longer as partners. They may not be quite as affectionate as some other toy-sized dogs, but they are still very loving and loyal. They are going to want to stay with you, and you can help keep them mentally engaged by teaching them tricks. This will keep them from getting too excited or wanting to do things they shouldn't do. Intelligent dogs have to be kept from getting bored to keep them from getting into trouble. You will almost certainly encounter some stubbornness, but you will need to work through it with patience and care. Your Pom wants to learn, but has to learn to respect and listen to you first, just like a child.

CHAPTER 3.
Finding Your Pomeranian

"Choosing the right Pomeranian can be hard, but adopting from the right breeder can help you out tremendously. By asking lots of questions, you can build a relationship with the breeder and understand their practices. This will help the breeder see what kind of puppy would be a good fit and you can get a better judgment on whether you'd like to do business with this breeder or not."

Fatihah Mach
Lunar Poms

Photo Courtesy of Jovanna D'Errico

CHAPTER 3   Finding Your Pomeranian

Having reached this chapter, you've probably decided you are up for the challenge and enjoyment of having such a large personality in such a small package.

We do not recommend that you purchase your new family member from a pet store or online. Do not meet along the side of the road to receive your new Pomeranian. You need to know the history of the parents and your dog so that you and your new friend will enjoy many happy and healthy years together. Like every other purebred dog, Pomeranians are prone to genetic problems because of inbreeding. By learning more about your dog's parents, you can ensure that you have the best odds for a healthy, happy Pomeranian.

Puppy Versus Adult

After you have decided you want a Pom, you need to consider which age is right for you. Adopting a puppy from a breeder is much different than rescuing a dog, and they each come with their own positive and negative aspects. Some of the considerations are universal, but there are a few extra considerations for Pomeranians because of their intellect and personalities.

Adopting A Puppy

Puppies are always a lot of work, and it begins even before the puppy reaches your home. You will need to spend weeks hunting for a reputable breeder and asking questions. Puppy proofing the home is as time consuming as child proofing your home, and you still have to keep a constant eye on your puppy. Training an intelligent breed like a Pom will be frustrating, and they are known to be difficult when it comes to housetraining. If you don't have the patience for a puppy that continually has accidents in the house, the Pom is not a good choice for you. You are pretty much going to need to be around for most of those early months to fully train and reinforce the training.

Expect to be on a waitlist; sometimes it can take over a year to get your puppy.

Puppies are even more fragile than the still fragile adults. You have to be very careful and make sure that no one tries to pick up your puppy, which is quite difficult because of how similar they are to stuffed animals in appearance. Other than their intelligence (which can hinder training) and their delicate bodies, you can expect your puppy to be relatively similar to raising any other dog breed.

Photo Courtesy of Shania Huge

CHAPTER 3   Finding Your Pomeranian

On the plus side, you will have many years more with your Pom than if you rescue an adult. You will have records about the puppy and the puppy's parents, making it easier to identify the potential problems your Pomeranian may suffer. This makes it considerably easier to ensure your puppy stays healthy and to catch potential issues earlier. If your puppy begins to display signs of any of the genetic problems, good breeders have contracts and guarantees (we will cover these a bit later). If the puppy is suffering from a genetic condition, the breeder will either refund your money or give you a new puppy.

Some people find it easier to bond with puppies than adult dogs. A young puppy is going to be nervous in a new home, but there isn't much risk of the puppy being dangerously aggressive. Your primary job will be in protecting your puppy and making sure that you patiently train it. Training is absolutely essential with Poms because of how intelligent they are, so you will need to have a plan in place before your puppy arrives. We will cover this more in a later chapter – for now, just make sure you understand that you are going to need a lot more time to train a puppy.

Rescuing A Pom

Rescuing any dog comes with some inherent risks, but it is a completely different set than bringing home a puppy. While it is possible to find Pom puppies at rescue places, it is much more likely that you will find an adult. Depending on the dog's age, you may need to reference both the pros and cons of both adopting a puppy and rescuing a dog.

As stated before, Poms are intelligent, stubborn, and fearless. This can make them difficult to adopt at a later age. Adults who were not properly trained or socialized can be real nightmares. Many Pom rescue organizations are going to be much more cautious about adopting out a rescue with personality and socialization issues. Rescue shelters will be less careful, though they will definitely try to impress upon potential adopters the risks and problems they are likely to face with a specific Pom in their care.

Poms may suffer from small dog syndrome, they could be nearly incurable barkers, or they could be completely untrained. All of these will make it far more difficult to train your rescue dog than if you adopt a puppy. Before you can begin to train an adult in many of the desired behaviors, you have to train out the undesirable behaviors. Essentially, you are starting from a negative space instead of a blank slate.

The benefits of rescuing a Pom are very similar to adopting any rescue dog. Many of them aren't bad dogs, they just have some bad habits. Odds are very good that you aren't going to be starting from scratch with

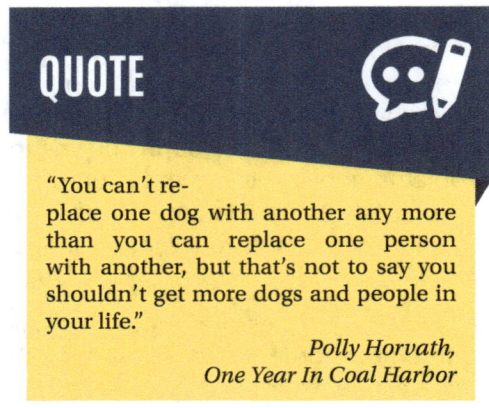

QUOTE

"You can't replace one dog with another any more than you can replace one person with another, but that's not to say you shouldn't get more dogs and people in your life."

Polly Horvath,
One Year In Coal Harbor

housetraining – which can be a huge plus for most people who don't have time to train a stubborn puppy. They are awake more often than puppies, and while it may take them a bit longer to warm up to you, you can bond much faster with an adult, depending on their age.

One thing that is similar to puppies is that you will want to puppy proof your home for a rescue. There is no telling what your dog does or doesn't know. If you have other dogs, you will probably want to have an area for your new Pom, but it will need to be bigger. Instead of setting up a small corner of a room though, you can make it a full room for your adult Pom. Make sure to have everything set up before the dog arrives – most people think it isn't necessary for an adult dog and fail to properly prepare. Don't think that rescuing a dog means you can skip this part. It will just be less time consuming than preparing a home for a puppy.

You may not be able to get a complete health record for a Pom that you adopt, but it is more likely that you will find a dog that has already been spayed or neutered, as well as being chipped. Unless you adopt a Pom that has health issues (these should be disclosed by the rescue organization), rescues tend to be less costly at the vet than puppies.

Older dogs give you more immediate gratification. You don't have to go through those sleepless nights with the new puppy or the endless frustration that comes with early types of training. Older Pomeranians let you get right into enjoying your dog as you go out on adventures. All intelligent, high-energy dogs require a lot of time and attention as puppies. Bypassing that is a major part of the appeal of older dogs.

Pomeranian Clubs And Rescues

Regardless of if you adopt a puppy or rescue an older Pom, you are going to need some familiarity with the different organizations that focus on Pomeranians. The best breeders will be part of these associations, which means that they have to meet a number of requirements and show that they are dedicated to raising and offering customers the healthiest possible puppies. Many of the organizations also work as rescue shelters. They will be able to provide you more information about each Pom they have up for

CHAPTER 3 Finding Your Pomeranian

adoption, as well as assessing you and your situation to determine if you and the Poms they have are a good match. The following are some of the most active organizations (most of which are Pomeranian specific) that can help you find a great breeder or a fantastic Pom to rescue.

- American Pomeranian Club
- Pawsitively Pom Rescue
- Pomeranian Rescue Group
- Recycled Pomeranians & Schipperkes Rescue
- Rescue Me! Pomeranian Rescue
- American Kennel Club (for additional Pomeranian breeders and rescues)

Photo Courtesy of Debbie Deardorf

Adopting From A Breeder

The health problems for Pomeranians are well documented. Breeders should be well aware of the risks and should be taking precautions to prevent the inherited ailments from being passed along to the puppies. Proper breeding and tracking of the parents can help to breed puppies that are far less likely to suffer from the ailments that are common in Pomeranians.

Health Tests And Certifications

Pomeranians have such a singular and long history that their genetics are very well documented. It also means that they are certain to have a number of genetic issues, though the issues are somewhat different since their history is several hundred years old on two very different continents.

To start, you need to know what kinds of health problems Pomeranians tend to have. The following are the health tests for Pomeranians:

- Patella evaluation
- Cardiac exam (OFA evaluation)
- Eye examination by someone who is a member of the ACVO Ophthalmologist (they should be registered with either the OFA or the CERF)

Breeders who are members of a Pomeranian association, club, or organization mentioned earlier in the chapter are already showing that they are serious about ensuring their dogs and puppies are healthy. Being a member of a Pomeranian organization requires that a set of requirements are being met, so it shows that they are reliable and predictable in the way they treat the puppies.

Contracts And Guarantees

Pomeranians really have not lost their popularity since the Victorian era, so it can be difficult to track all of the genetics. The contracts and guarantees are meant to protect the puppies as much as they are meant to protect you.

If a breed has a contract that must be signed, make sure that you read through it completely and are willing to meet all of the requirements prior to signing it. The contracts tend to be fairly easy to understand and comply with, but you should be aware of all of the facts before you agree to anything. Beyond putting down the money for the puppy, signing the contract says that you are serious about how you plan to take care of the puppy to

CHAPTER 3 Finding Your Pomeranian

Photo Courtesy of Melanie Adkins

the best of your abilities by meeting the minimum requirements set forth by the breeder. Since the contracts focus on your behavior toward taking care of your dog, it is a good sign that breeders want to verify that you are serious about taking care of your puppy. It is probable that the contract will include spaying or neutering the puppy once it matures (typically six months). It may also say that the breeder will retain the registration papers of the puppy, although you can get a copy of them.

The guarantee states what health conditions the breeder guarantees for their puppies. This typically includes details of the dog's health and recommendations on the next steps of the puppy's care once it leaves the breeder's home. Guarantees may also provide schedules to ensure that the health care started by the breeder is continued by the new puppy parent. In the event that a major health concern is found, the puppy will need to be returned to the breeder. The contract will also explain what is not guaranteed. The guarantee tends to be very long (sometimes longer than the contract), and you should read it thoroughly before you sign the contract. Guarantees are fairly common with Pomeranians because of how old the breed is. The guarantees state what the breeder is guaranteeing with your new dog. This usually includes information on the dog's health and recommendations on what the pet owner's next steps should be. For example, it may recommend that you take your puppy to the vet within two days of arriving at your home to ensure the dog is as healthy as it is believed to be.

In addition to the price of getting your dog, Pomeranian contracts ensure certain behavior by the new human parent of a Pomeranian puppy. The contract may also contain naming requirements, health details, and a stipulation for what will happen if you can no longer take care of the canine (the dog usually goes back to the breeder). They also include information on what will happen if you are negligent or abusive.

Puppy Genetics – The Parents

A healthy puppy requires having healthy parents and a clean genetic history. Finding a good breeder means finding a breeder that has kept extensive records of each puppy (and their parents depending on how long breeders have been breeding dogs). You will want to review each of the parents' complete history to understand what traits your puppy is likely to inherit. Pay attention to their learning abilities, temperament, clinginess, and any personality trait you consider important. You can either request documents be sent electronically or when you visit the breeder in person.

CHAPTER 3   Finding Your Pomeranian

It could take a while to review the breeder's information about each parent, but it is always well worth the time you spend studying and planning for the puppy. The more you know about the parents, the better prepared you will be for your puppy. The great breeders will have stories and details about the parents so that you can read about them at your leisure, as well as getting a good feel for the breeders.

Breeders should be concerned with breeding out potential genetic health conditions, which will be reflected in the documentation about the parents. You can see if the parents have displayed problems, if their siblings or parents had genetic issues, and if their puppies have presented any of the health risks.

> **HELPFUL TIP**
> **Royal Pomeranian**
>
> Queen Charlotte, wife of King George III of England, originated from a German territory near Pomerania. When Charlotte came to England to marry George in 1761, she brought her Pomeranians with her. Queen Victoria, granddaughter of Queen Charlotte, also had a great love of Pomeranians. Queen Victoria's kennel at Windsor Castle housed more than 30 Pomeranians which she had imported from around Europe.

Finding A Breeder

Now that you know some of the basics of what to expect, it is time to start talking to breeders. The goal of these phone calls is to determine which breeders are willing to take the time to answer all of your questions, provide all of the necessary information, and really take care of the parents and the puppies. They should have as much love for their Pomeranians as they want you to feel for your new puppy. And they should want to make sure that their puppies go to good homes.

The first thing you need to do when looking for the right breeder is to look for someone who clearly loves the dogs and is willing to put in the extra effort and attention to raise them right. They should begin some of the initial training too, training that will prepare the puppies for life. If you find someone who posts regular pictures and information about the parents and the progress of the mother's pregnancy and vet visits, that is a very good sign. The best breeders will not only talk about their dogs and the plans for the parents in the future, they will stay in contact with you after you take the puppy home and answer any questions as they arise. These are the kinds of breeders who are likely to have waiting lists and posts about their puppies and the information their new families provide. The active interest in knowing about what happens to the puppies later shows that they care a great deal about each individual dog.

You will need to plan for hours of research and prepare a list of questions for each of the breeders you talk to. It is likely that for each breeder you call, the conversation will last about an hour. That is for each breeder you contact. If a breeder does not have time to talk and isn't willing to talk with you later, you can cross them off of your list. After you have talked with each of your possible breeders, compare their answers. With a breed like the Pomeranian, there are some variations in personalities based on what the parents are like. If you want a dog that is more easily trained, you want parents that are more intelligent and less stubborn to increase the likelihood that your puppy will be easier to train.

The following are some questions to ask. Make sure that you have pen and paper or your computer handy.

- Ask if you can visit in person. The answer should always be yes, and if it isn't, you don't need to ask any further. Thank them and hang up. Even if the breeder is located in a different state, they should allow you to visit them. You should definitely make an attempt to visit them (and that is why we recommend you look for a reputable local breeder before looking further from home).
- Ask about the required health tests and certifications they have for their puppies. These points are detailed further in the next section, so make sure to check off the available tests and certifications for each breeder. If they don't have all of the tests and certifications, you may want to remove them from consideration. Good breeders not only cover all of these points, they offer a guarantee against the most harmful genetic issues.
- Make sure that the breeder always takes care of all of the initial health requirements in the first few weeks through the early months, particularly shots. Puppies require that certain procedures be started before they leave their mother to ensure they are healthy. Vaccinations and worming typically start around six weeks after the puppies are born, then need to be continued every three weeks. By the time your puppy is old enough to come home, the puppy should be well into the procedures, or even completely through with the first phases of these important health care needs.
- Ask if the puppy is required to be spayed or neutered before reaching a certain age of maturity. It is possible that you may need to sign a contract that says you will have the procedure done, which you will need

CHAPTER 3   Finding Your Pomeranian

to plan for prior to getting your puppy. Typically, these procedures are done in the puppies' best interest.

- Find out if the breeder is part of a Pomeranian organization or group.
- Ask about the first phases of your puppy's life, such as how the breeder plans to care for the puppy during those first few months. They should be able to provide a lot of detail, and they should do this without sounding as though they are irritated that you want to know. They will also let you know how much training you can expect to be done prior to the puppy's arrival in your home so you can plan to take over as soon as the puppy arrives. It is possible that the breeders typically start housetraining (in which case, you are very lucky if you can get on the waiting list with them). You will also want to find out if they can provide information on how the puppies have been performing and how quickly they have picked up on the training. You want to be able to pick up from where the breeder left off once your Pomeranian reaches your home.
- See what kind of advice the breeder gives about raising your Pomeranian puppy. They should be more than happy to help guide you to doing what is best for your dog because they will want the puppies to live happy, healthy lives even after leaving the breeder's home. You want a caring breeder who is more interested in the health of the puppies than in the money they make. You should definitely expect to pay more, but you should also get recommendations, advice, and additional care after the puppy arrives at your home. Basically, you are getting customer support, as well as a great chance of raising a healthy dog. Breeders who show a lot of interest in the dog's well-being and are willing to answer questions during the dog's entire life span are likely to breed puppies that are healthy.
- How many breeds do they manage a year? How many sets of parents do the breeders have? Puppies can take a lot of time and attention, and the mother should have some down time between pregnancies. Learn about the breeder's standard operations to find out if they are taking care of the parents and treating them like valuable family members and not as strictly a way to make money.

Selecting Your Puppy

"The puppy should be friendly, but not too shy or too aggressive. An old breeder I knew that has now passed on, said if you want to know if a puppy is for you, just hold it a while and if it settles down a sighs a big sigh, he or she has chosen you."

Claudia Wallen
Pearl Moon Poms

Selecting your puppy should be done in person. However, you can start checking out the puppies after birth if the breeder is willing to share videos and pictures. When you are finally allowed to check out the puppies in person, there are several things you need to check the puppies for before making your final decision. Some of the things that you are looking are universal, regardless of the breed, and other things are Pomeranian specific.

- Check out the group of puppies as a whole. If most or all of the puppies are aggressive or fearful, this is an indication of a problem with the litter or (more likely) the breeder. Here are a few red flags if displayed by a majority of the puppies:
  - Tucked tails
  - Shrinking away from people
  - Whimpering when people get close
  - Constant attacking of your hands or feet (beyond pouncing)
- If you have dogs at home, notice how well each puppy plays with the others. This is a great indicator of just how well your puppy will react to any pets you already have.
- Notice which puppies greet you first, and which hang back to observe. Keep in mind that the puppy or puppies that greet you are more forward and demanding than the ones that sit back and analyze the situation first.
- The puppies should not be fat or underweight, which admittedly can be difficult to tell with their coats. A swollen stomach is generally a sign of worms or other health problems.
- Puppies should have straight legs that are sturdy. Splayed legs can be a sign that there is something wrong.

CHAPTER 3 Finding Your Pomeranian

- Examine the puppy's ears for mites, which will cause discharge in the ears. The inside should be pink, not red or inflamed.
- The eyes should be clear and bright.
- Check the puppy's mouth for pink, healthy-looking gums.
- Pet the puppy to check their coats for the following.
    - Ensure that coat feels thick and full. If the breeders have allowed the fur to get matted or really dirty, it is an indication that they likely are not taking proper care of the puppy.
    - Check for fleas and mites by running your hand from the head to the tail, then under the tail (fleas are more likely to hide under most dogs' tails). Mites may look like dandruff.
- Check the puppy's rump for redness and sores, and see if you can check the last bowel movement to ensure it is firm.

Pick the puppy that exhibits the personality traits that you want in your dog. If you want a forward, friendly, excitable dog, the first puppy to greet you may be the one you seek. If you want a dog that will think things through and let others get more attention, this is mellower dog that may be better for your home.

CHAPTER 4.
Preparing For Your Puppy

Preparing for a puppy is far more time consuming than preparing for an adult dog. Most adult dogs are already knowledgeable about what it is like to live in a home. That doesn't mean you won't have a considerable amount of preparation for an adult, but you aren't going to be puppy-proofing pretty much everything.

It takes months to prepare a home for a puppy, and there is still plenty to do during those last few weeks. There is so much to do, it can easily get overwhelming, or you can get carried away, buying far more than is necessary for your puppy. What you need to do is sit down and plan for your puppy's arrival. Be prepared for it to take about as long as if you were bringing a baby into the home, with many of the same concerns. Of course it isn't the most enjoyable task, but it is important to make your home as safe as possible. Making sure your new Pomeranian has a safe space with all of the essentials (especially the toys) will make the arrival of your newest family addition a great time for everyone – especially your new canine companion.

CHAPTER 4   Preparing For Your Puppy

Preparing Your Kids

Pomeranians are as delicate as they are adorable. This is why you should not consider the breed if you have young children – trying to get children to understand that they need to be gentle can be incredibly difficult. You will have your work cut out for you getting older children and teenagers to understand to be careful. Of course, you have time to prepare them and to put the rules of puppy-play in place.

FUN FACT
Lap of Luxury

In 2014, Paris Hilton purchased a micro Pomeranian named Mr. Amazing who was advertised as the world's smallest Pomeranian. Mr. Amazing was listed as 10 ounces and reportedly sold for $13,000.

Begin to prepare your kids as soon as you plan to adopt your Pomeranian – even if you plan to get an adult. Preparing your children will be a bit different based on their age, but the same rules will need to apply regardless of the age of your children. Then there are the aspects of preparing them that are universal, regardless of age.

You will need to be ready to refresh these rules regularly, both before the puppy arrives and after the arrival. The first time your kids begin to play with the puppy, you will need to be present, and you cannot leave them alone. You will actually need to stay with your children when they interact with the puppy for several months, or longer, depending on the kids' age. Older teens will probably be all right to help with the puppy, but younger teens and kids should not be left alone with the puppy for a few months. Remember that you will need to be very firm to make sure that the puppy is not hurt.

The following are the five golden rules that you want to make sure your children follow from the very first interaction.
1. Always be gentle.
2. Chase is an outside game.
3. Always leave the puppy alone during mealtime.
4. The Pomeranian should always remain firmly on the ground.
5. All of your valuables should be well out of reach of your children, even your teens.

Photo Courtesy of Rachel Lubbe

CHAPTER 4   Preparing For Your Puppy

Since your kids are going to ask why, here are the explanations you can give them. You can simplify them for younger kids, or start a dialogue with teens.

Always Be Gentle

Those little Pomeranians are absolutely adorable, but they are also fairly fragile, despite their fluffy appearance. At no time should anyone play rough with the puppy (or any adult Pomeranian).

This rule must be applied consistently every time your children play with the puppy. Be firm if you see your children getting too excited or rough. You don't want the puppy to get overly excited either because puppies may end up nipping or biting. It isn't their fault because they haven't learned better yet – it is the child's fault. Make sure your child understands the possible repercussions if they get too rough.

Chase

It can be easy for children to forget as they start to play and everyone gets excited. That short game of getting away can quickly devolve into chase, so you will need to make sure your children understand not to start running. Once they get outside, chase is perfectly fine (though you will still need to monitor the playtime).

Running inside the home is dangerous for two primary reasons. It gives your Pomeranian puppy the impression that your home isn't safe inside because they are being chased, or worse, they get hurt. Or your puppy will learn that running inside is fine, which can be very dangerous as they get older. One of the last things you want is for your Pomeranian to go barreling through your home knocking into people's feet because it was fine for them to do that when they were puppies.

Mealtime

This is true whenever your puppy is eating (this can apply to when your kids are eating as well since you don't want your Pomeranian to get accustomed to eating people food when your kids are eating). You don't want your Pomeranian to think that anyone is trying to take the food away. Pomeranians aren't typically aggressive, so it isn't likely they will nip or bite because someone is near their food. However, they can feel insecure about eating if they feel like someone may take their food away, which is obviously not fair to your Pomeranian. And older Pomeranians could be a bit more protective of their food, which could lead to some conflicts. Save yourself,

Photo Courtesy of Debra Geist

your family, and your Pomeranian trouble by making sure everyone knows that eating time is your Pomeranian's time alone.

Paws On The Ground

This is something that will likely require a good bit of explaining to your children as Pomeranians look a lot like toys, especially Pomeranian puppies. No one should be picking the puppy up off the ground. You may want to carry your new family member around or play with the pup like a baby, but you and your family will need to resist that urge. Kids particularly have trouble understanding since they will see the Pomeranian more like a toy than a living creature. The younger your children are, the more difficult it will be for them to understand the difference. It is so tempting to treat the Pomeranian like a baby and to try to carry it like one, but this is incredibly uncomfortable and unhealthy for the canine. Older kids will quickly learn that a puppy nip or bite hurts a lot more than you would think. Those little teeth are incredibly sharp, and you do not want the puppy to be dropped. If your children learn never to pick up the puppy, things will go a lot better. Remember, this also applies to you, so don't make things difficult by doing something you constantly tell your children not to do.

Valuables Out Of Reach

Valuables are not something you want to end up in the puppy's mouth, but that is almost guaranteed to happen if you leave jewelry where someone can easily pick it up. Teenagers are just as likely to grab whatever is within easy reach to play with the puppy, so they are nearly as much of a threat to your valuables as tweens and kids who are older than toddlers. If your kids get curious, they are not likely to stop to consider if they should be doing something because they want to know what will happen if they use a particular item to play with the puppy. The end result will be an incident that will certainly not make you happy, nor your children when you get upset with them. If you don't want your puppy or children to destroy something valuable, make sure it is never easily accessible.

Photo Courtesy of Krysta Lannan

CHAPTER 4   Preparing For Your Puppy

Preparing Your Current Dogs

"Do not assume that you're current dog that you've had forever will not harm the pup. When owners are not locking the current pet can show jealousy towards the Pom pup & have been known to hurt or kill the Pom pup."

Gary & Janie Burnette
Burnette's Exclusive Pomeranians

If you already have canines in your home, they are going to need to be prepared too, but it is going to be vastly different than preparing kids. You can't tell a dog what is coming, but your dog is going to notice the changes you are making to the home. Once your children understand the rules, you will need to start working on making your dog feel secure.

Here are the important tasks to prepare your current pets for your new arrival.
- Set a schedule for the things you will need to do and the people who will need to participate.
- Preserve your dogs' favorite places and furniture, and make sure their toys and items are not in the puppy's space.
- Have play dates at your home and analyze your dogs to see how they react.

Set A Schedule

During this time, you are going to be establishing a schedule that you will keep once the puppy arrives. This lets your furry companion know that they are still loved after a puppy arrives. Obviously, the puppy is going to get a lot of attention, so you need to make a concerted effort to let your current canine know that you still love and care for him. Basically, you are making time in your schedule just for your dog or dogs, and you will need to make sure that you don't stray from that schedule after the puppy's arrival.

Make sure that you plan to have at least one adult around for each other dog you have. Cats are generally less of a concern, but you will probably want to have at least one other adult around when the puppy comes home. We will go into more detail later about what the roles of the other adults will be, but for now, when you know what date you will be bringing your puppy home, make sure that you have adults who know to be present to help. You may need to remind them as the time nears too, so set an alert on your phone for that, as well as the date, time, and pickup information for your puppy.

Leaving Your Dogs' Important Toys And Space Alone

If you do have a dog, you are going to need to be careful about where you put your puppy's space because you should not keep your dog from the areas if they are your dog's favorite places. This is because you are going to be fencing in the area so that your other dogs cannot get into the puppy's space. Your puppy is going to eat, sleep, and spend most of the day and night in the space. This means that the space cannot block your current canine from favorite furniture, bed, or any place where your dog rests over the course of the day. None of your dog's stuff should be in this area, and this includes pulling all of your dog's toys from the area. You don't

Photo Courtesy of Roberta Slagle

CHAPTER 4 Preparing For Your Puppy

Photo Courtesy of Cassie Revett

want your dog to feel like the puppy is taking over his territory. Make sure your children understand to never to put your dog's stuff in the puppy's area as well.

Your dog and the puppy will need to be kept apart in the early days, (even if they seem friendly) until your puppy is done with vaccinations. Puppies are more susceptible to illness during these days, so wait until the puppy is protected before the dogs spend time together. This means that the designated puppy space should be somewhere that your dog is not likely to miss – it should not be near your dog's favorite furniture or resting spots.

Getting An Idea How Your Dogs Will React – Extra At Home Play Dates

Here are the things that will best help prepare your pooch for the arrival of your puppy.

- Think about your dog's personality to help you decide the best way to prepare for that first day, week, and month. Each dog is unique, so you will need to consider your dog's personality to determine how things will go when the new dog arrives. If your dog loves other dogs, this will probably hold true when the puppy shows up. If your dog has any territorial tendencies, you will need to be cautious during the introduction and first couple of months so your current dog learns that the Pomeranian is now a part of the pack. Excitable dogs will need special attention to keep them from getting overly excited when a new dog comes home. You don't want them to be so excited they accidentally hurt the new Pomeranian.

- Consider the times when you have had other dogs in your home and how your dog reacted to these other furry visitors. If your canine displayed territorial tendencies, you are going to need to be extra careful with how you introduce your new pup. If you haven't invited another dog to your home, you need to have a couple of play dates with other dogs at your home before your new Pomeranian arrives. You have to know how your current furry babies will react to new dogs in the house so you can properly prepare. Meeting a dog at home is very different from encountering one outside the home.

- Think about your dog's interactions with other dogs for as long as you have known the pup. Has your dog shown either protective or possessive behavior, either with you or others? Food is one of the reasons most dogs will display some kind of aggression because they don't want anyone trying to eat what is theirs. Some dogs can be protective of people and toys too.

The same rules apply, no matter how many dogs you have. Think about the personalities of all of them as individuals, as well as how they interact together. Just like people, you may find that when they are together your dogs act differently, which you will need to keep in mind as you plan their first introduction.

See chapter 9 for planning to introduce your current dogs and your new puppy, and how to juggle a new puppy and your current canine or canines.

CHAPTER 4   Preparing For Your Puppy

Photo Courtesy of Stacey Papo

Dangerous Foods

The way your dog processes food is not identical to how you process food. They can eat raw meat without having to worry about the kinds of problems a person will encounter. However, there are foods that you can process without concern that could be fatal to your Pomeranian. Given how small they are, it does not take much of these kinds of foods to kill a Pomeranian. While you should keep these foods away from all dogs, you need to be particularly careful not to let your Pomeranian eat these foods:

- Apple seeds
- Chocolate
- Coffee
- Cooked bones (they can kill a dog when the bones splinter in the dog's mouth or stomach)

Photo Courtesy of
Daphne Meng
Countryside Pomeranians

CHAPTER 4   Preparing For Your Puppy

- Corn on the cob (it is the cob that is deadly to dogs; corn off the cob is fine, but you need to make sure your Pomeranian cannot reach any corn that is still on the cob)
- Grapes/raisins
- Macadamia nuts
- Onions and chives
- Peaches, persimmons, and plums
- Tobacco (your Pomeranian will not know that it is not a food and may eat it if left out)
- Xylitol (a sugar substitute in candies and baked goods)
- Yeast

In addition to these potentially deadly foods, there is a long list of things that your dog shouldn't eat for health reasons. The Canine Journal has a lengthy list of foods that should be avoided. It includes foods like alcohol and other things that people give dogs thinking it is funny. Remember that dogs have a very different metabolism and the effect that these foods have on them is much stronger than the effect they have on people.

For the sake of your Pomeranian's health, it is best just to keep all of these foods out of reach, even if the items are non-lethal.

Hazards To Fix

Preparing for a puppy is going to be time consuming, and all of the most dangerous rooms and items in your home will be equally dangerous to your puppy as they are to a baby. The biggest difference is that your Pomeranian is going to be mobile much faster than a child, potentially getting into dangerous situations within a few weeks if you don't take care to secure all of the dangers ahead of your puppy's arrival.

For the month or three leading up to your puppy's arrival, you are going to be puppy proofing your home. It is going to require a considerable amount of time, so make sure you set aside at least a month (more time is better) to get your home puppy ready. The time you put into making your home safe for the puppy is well worth any extra effort.

Be aware that Pomeranians (and puppies in general) will try to eat virtually anything, even if it isn't food. Nothing is safe – not even your furniture. Puppies will gnaw on wood and metal. Anything else within their reach is fair game. Keep this in mind as you go about puppy-proofing your home.

Indoor Fixes

This section details the areas inside your home where you should really focus your attention. In case of problems, have your vet's number posted to the fridge and in at least one other room in the house. If you set this up before your pup arrives, it will be there if you need it. Even if you program it into your phone, another family member or someone taking care of your Pom may need the number.

Hazards	Fixes	Time Estimate
Kitchen		
Poisons	Keep in secured, childproofed cabinets or on high shelves	30 min
Trash cans	Have a lockable trash can, or keep it in a secured location	10 min
Appliances	Make sure all cords are out of reach	15 min
Food	Keep it out of reach and never hanging over the side of surfaces	Constant (start making it a habit)
Floors		
Slippery surfaces	Put down rugs or one of the special mats that is designed to stick to the floor	30 min – 1 hour
Training area	Train on non-slippery surfaces	Constant
Bathrooms		
Toilet brush	Either have one that locks or keep it out of reach	5 min/bathroom
Poisons	Keep in secured, childproofed cabinets or on high shelves	15 - 30 min/ bathroom
Toilets	Keep closed	
Do not use automatic-toilet chemicals	Constant (start making it a habit)	
Cabinets	Keep locked with childproof locks	15 - 30 min/ bathroom
Laundry Room		
Clothing	Store clean and dirty clothing off the floor, out of reach	15 – 30 min

CHAPTER 4   Preparing For Your Puppy

Poisons (bleach, pods/ detergent, dryer sheets, and misc. poisons)	Keep in secured, childproofed cabinets or on high shelves	15 min
Around the Home		
Plants	Keep off the ground	45 min – 1 hour
Trash cans	Have a lockable trash can, or keep it in a secured location	30 min
Electrical cords	Hide them or makes sure they are out of reach;	
pay particular attention to entertainment and computer areas	1.5 hours	
Poisons	Check to make sure there aren't any (WD40, window/ screen cleaner, carpet cleaner, air fresheners); move all poisons to a centralized, locked location	1 hour
Windows	Check that cords are out of reach in all rooms	1 – 2 hours
Fireplaces	Store cleaning supplies and tools where the puppy cannot get into them	
Cover the fireplace opening with something the puppy cannot knock over	10 min/fireplace	
Stairs	Cordoned off so that your puppy cannot try to go up or down them; make sure to test gates/blocks	10 – 15 min
Coffee tables/ End tables/ Nightstands	Clear of dangerous objects (e.g., scissors, sewing equipment, pens, and pencils) and all valuables	30 – 45 min

If you have a cat, keep the litter box off of the floor. It needs to be somewhere that your cat can easily go but your Pomeranian cannot. Since this could include teaching your cat to use the new area, it is something you should do well in advance of the puppy's arrival. You don't want your cat to be undergoing too many significant changes all at once. The puppy will

Photo Courtesy of Debbie Deardorf

be enough of a disruption – if your cat associates the litter box change with the puppy, you may find your cat protesting the change by refusing to use the litter box.

Pomeranians can get into nearly everything at their height, and they will be exploring a lot when given the opportunity. Anything that may catch your attention or draw your interest is worth a try – that's what centuries have taught them. Being vigilant about making sure they can't hurt themselves is vital to keeping your Pomeranian safe.

Remember, this is an intelligent breed, so your Pom is going to figure out how to do things you do not want the pup to do. This could range from getting into an open toilet (which is why you cannot have automatic-chemical rinses) to crawling into cabinets or pantries. While they may not be as intelligent as Corgis who can climb on furniture to eat meals, then hide their method of transgressing, Pomeranians aren't too far behind in their mental abilities. It is best to overestimate what they can do and to make sure that you adapt your habits before your puppy arrives.

Before you call it good, you are going to need to get low and see each room from your Pom's perspective. You are almost guaranteed to find at least one thing you missed.

Outdoor Fixes

This section details the things outside your home that need your attention ahead of your puppy's arrival. Also post the vet's number in one of the sheltered areas in case of an emergency.

Hazards	Fixes	Time Estimate
Garage		
Poisons	Keep in secured, childproofed cabinets or on high shelves (e.g., car chemicals, cleaning, paint, lawn care) – this includes fertilizer	1 hour
Trash bins	Keep them in a secured location	5 min
Tools (e.g., lawn, car, hardware, power tools)	Make sure all cords are out of reach: keep tools out of reach and never hanging over the side of surfaces	30 min – 1 hour
Equipment (e.g., sports, fishing)	Keep it out of reach and never hanging over the side of surfaces	Constant (start making it a habit)
Sharp implements	Keep them out of reach and never hanging over the side of surfaces	30 min
Bikes	Store them off the ground or in a place the Pom cannot go to keep the pup from biting the tires	20 min
Fencing (Can Be Done Concurrently)		
Breaks	Fix any breaks in the fencing	30 min - 1 hour
Gaps	Fill any gaps, even if they are intentional, so your Pom doesn't escape	30 min - 1 hour
Holes/Dips at Base	Fill any area that can be easily crawled under	1 – 2 hours
Yard		
Poisons	Don't leave any poisons in the yard	1 – 2 hours
Plants	Verify that all low plants aren't poisonous to dogs; fence off anything that is (such as grapevines)	45 min – 1 hour
Tools (e.g., lawn maintenance and gardening tools)	Make sure they are out of reach; make sure nothing is hanging over outdoor tables	30 min – 1 hour

Never leave your Pomeranian alone in the garage, even when it is an adult. It is likely that your puppy will be in the garage when you take car trips, which is why it is important to puppy proof it. You should always have an eye on the dog, but you obviously cannot climb under the car and will have a hard time getting into smaller spaces if your Pom makes a break for it to explore.

Yard preparation is going to be a bit different for such a small dog as a Pomeranian. You should definitely make the backyard safe, but you really shouldn't send your Pom out alone. They are small enough for larger birds of prey to pick up and for other wild animals to eat, making it very risky for them to go out alone.

Just like inside, you will need to follow up you preparations by getting low and checking out all areas from a small dog's perspective. Again, you are all but guaranteed to find at least one thing you missed.

Supplies And Tools To Purchase And Prepare

Planning for your puppy's arrival means buying a lot supplies up front. You will need a wide range of items. If you start making purchases around the time you identify the breeder, you can stretch out your expenses over a longer period of time. This will make it seem a lot less expensive than it actually is, though it is much cheaper than what is needed for most other breeds. The following are recommended items:

- Playpen (optional)
- Crate
- Bed
- Leash
- Doggy bags for walks
- Collar
- Tags
- Puppy food
- Water and food bowls (sharing a water bowl is usually okay, but your puppy needs his or her own food dish if you have multiple dogs)
- Toothbrush/Toothpaste
- Brush
- Toys

For training treats, you actually have it very easy. Instead of buying the more expensive treats, Cheerios are just as effective and much cheaper. One little piece of cereal for listening is all it takes, and your Pomeranian is not likely to get tired of eating them since this is not a breed that is particularly picky about food.

If there is anything else you want, feel free to add it to the list.

CHAPTER 4   Preparing For Your Puppy

Health care items like flea treatments can be purchased, but they are expensive and you won't need them for a while. Puppies should not be treated until they reach a specified age.

Choosing Your Vet

You can start looking around for a vet for your Pomeranian even before you choose a breeder. This is a task that you can do when you have time, but it must be done at least a few weeks before your Pom arrives. Whether you get a puppy or an adult, you should take your canine to the vet within 48 hours (24 hours is strongly recommended) of their arrival. Getting an appointment with a vet can take a while, just like getting a doctor's appointment, so you will need to have your vet and the first appointment booked well in advance.

Here are some things to consider when looking for a vet.
- What is their level of familiarity with Pomeranians? They don't have to be specialists, but you do want them to have some experience with the breed.
- How far from your home is the vet? You don't want the vet to be 30 minutes or more from your home.
- Is the vet available for emergencies or can they recommend a vet in case of an emergency?
- Is the vet part of a local vet hospital if needed, or does the doctor refer patients to a local pet hospital?
- Is the vet the only vet or one of several partners? If part of a partnership, can you stick with just one vet for visits?
- How are appointments booked?
- Can you have other services performed there, such as grooming and boarding?
- Is the vet accredited?
- What are the prices for the initial visit and the normal costs, such as shots and regular visits?
- What tests and checks are performed during the initial visit?

Make time to visit the vet you are considering using so that you can look around to see what the environment is inside. See if you can speak to the vet to see if he or she is willing to help put you at ease and answer your questions. Their time is valuable, but they have a few minutes to help you feel confident that they are the right choice to help take care of your canine.

Photo Courtesy of Jovanna D'Errico

CHAPTER 4   Preparing For Your Puppy

Planning The First Year's Budget

The budget for having a puppy is a lot more than you would think – it's still less expensive to bring in a puppy than a new infant. You will need to have a budget, which is another reason to start purchasing supplies a few months in advance. When you buy the items you need, you will begin to see exactly how much you will spend a month. Of course there are some items that are one-time purchases, such as the crate, but many other items you will need to purchase regularly, like food and treats.

You also need to have a budget for the one-time purchases. This means doing some research ahead of time for those purchases. It is almost guaranteed that you are going to overspend, but you will want to stick to the budget as much as possible.

Begin budgeting the day you decide to get your puppy. The cost will include the adoption cost, which is typically higher for a purebred dog than for a rescue. If you want to rescue a Pomeranian, you should figure out where you want to find your newest family member. Plan to spend a lot of time researching costs for bringing your puppy or adult dog home, as well as the other costs.

The vet and other healthcare costs should be included in your budget. Regular vaccinations are required, and an annual checkup should be included in the budget. Vet prices vary a lot between different states, even between cities, making it difficult to average the cost. It is always worth the cost, but you will want to know what the cost will be before your puppy arrives.

If you want to join a Pomeranian organization, budget for the activities. There are a lot of things you can do with Pomeranians if you want to be with other puppy parents. Fortunately, this is not necessary because Pomeranians love to lounge at home and don't require much time outside of the home to be perfectly content.

CHAPTER 5.
Bringing Home Your Pomeranian

"I strongly suggest that a new puppy be treated the same as bringing home a newborn baby. Do not leave them alone for the first couple of weeks. I recommend you have a sitter lined up if you have to work or leave."

Kim Howard
TK Kennels

The first week with your Pomeranian is going to be incredible, tiring, and all kinds of entertaining and frustrating. It will be very similar to that first week after you bring a newborn home, with many of the same things to make you smile and to keep you up at night. Years later, you are still going to remember what it was like when your puppy first arrived. You probably won't remember as much about later in the week as you find that you are getting less sleep. Your Pomeranian is going to be so adorable and cuddly that you will quickly realize that you don't want to return to a time before your puppy was there. The work is more than worth it.

CHAPTER 5 Bringing Home Your Pomeranian

Final Preparations And Planning

Make sure you have taken time off of work or that you will be 100% at home during at least the first 24 hours, if not the first 48 hours to a week. Your new puppy is going to need you, so as much time as you can dedicate in those first few days will be best for your newest family member.

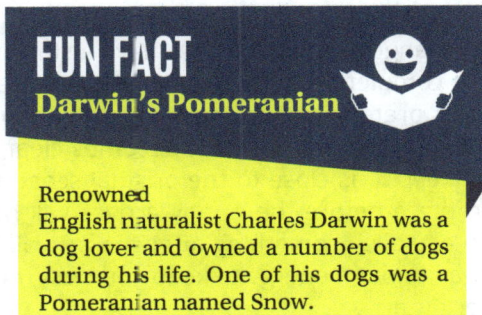

FUN FACT
Darwin's Pomeranian

Renowned English naturalist Charles Darwin was a dog lover and owned a number of dogs during his life. One of his dogs was a Pomeranian named Snow.

You've already seen that there are a lot of plans and preparations that need to be made, but preparing the house is just one of the important tasks. To ensure you finish everything, create a couple of checklists, including one to review just before bringing your puppy home. Once your puppy is in your home, you really are not going to have time to do anything apart from taking care of your puppy.

From the puppy area to puppy supplies, you want to make sure you have everything you need several days before the puppy's arrival. The following are essentials, though you can add anything else you feel you should buy so that you don't have to run out and buy them last minute or after your puppy is already getting familiar with the home:

- Food
- Bed
- Crate
- Toys
- Water and food dishes
- Leash
- Collar
- Treats

All of these items should be set up and ready for use before the puppy arrives. You aren't going to have time to do anything besides taking care of that puppy.

You also should have a checklist for inspecting your home to make sure there are no dangers just before your puppy arrives. Set time to go over the inspection checklist a couple of hours before the arrival. That will help you better enjoy your time with your newest family addition.

If you plan to have a fence to keep the puppy penned into a specific area of the home, have the gates set up and verify that they cannot be knocked over or circumvented. Your Pomeranian is probably going to try to make a break for it if there are any weaknesses or holes in the fencing around his designated area. A playpen will actually be easier and your puppy isn't going to mind.

Set up a schedule for the puppy's care. Know that the plans are going to change, but you need to have a starting point. This will ensure that people complete their assigned tasks and help to make your puppy feel safe – dogs prefer structure, so schedules are a great source of security for them. Tweak the schedule as it becomes clear that changes are needed, but try to keep it as close to the original schedule as possible. Having a schedule in place before the puppy arrives will make it a lot easier than if you try to establish something after the arrival. The canine is going to have more than enough energy to keep you busy, making it difficult to make a plan after his arrival.

The schedule should include a bathroom break after every meal. There is a good chance your puppy will need to go then, and this will help establish where the right places are to use the bathroom.

Have a final meeting with all of the family members to make sure all of the rules are remembered and understood before the puppy is a distraction. Children will need special training in how to handle the puppy, and you are going to need to be very strict in making sure they aren't too rough with the pup. Verify that your children understand that they are not allowed to play with the puppy unless there is an adult supervising them. Determine who is going to be responsible for primary puppy care, including who will be the primary trainer. To help teach younger children about responsibility, a parent can pair with a child to manage the puppy's care. The child will be responsible for things like keeping the water bowl filled and feeding the puppy, and a parent can oversee the tasks.

Puppy training happens from the moment your Pomeranian is under your care. The rules and hierarchy should start to be established from that first car ride home.

As tempting as it is to cuddle and try to make the ride comfortable, using a crate for the ride is both safer and more comfortable – you cannot start by making an exception. Your puppy is learning from the very beginning. Remember, this is a breed that has been living alongside humans for a very long time, and they know how to take cues from you. Anything that they can do to make you drop your guard and let them get away with stuff, they are going to use later. As difficult as it will be, you will need to be firm and consistent with your Pomeranian.

CHAPTER 5 Bringing Home Your Pomeranian

The Ride Home

Before leaving, make sure you have everything you need prepared.
- The crate should be anchored with a cushion to make the trip safe.
- Call to make sure everything is still on schedule and make sure the puppy is ready.
- Ask, if you haven't already, if you can get the mother to leave her scent on a blanket to help make the puppy's transition more comfortable.
- Make sure your other adult remembers and will be on time to head to the pickup destination.
- If you have dogs, make sure that all adults know what to do and where to go for that first neutral meeting.

Two adults should be present on the first trip. Ask the breeder if the puppy has been in a car before, and, if not, it is especially important to have someone who can give the puppy attention while the other person drives. The puppy will be in the crate, but someone can still provide comfort. It will definitely be scary because the puppy no longer has mom, siblings, or known people around, so having someone present to talk to the puppy will make it a little less of an ordeal for the little guy. Pomeranians may not be a fearful breed, but that doesn't mean they don't get scared when they are young.

This is the time to start teaching your puppy that car trips are enjoyable. This means making sure that the crate is secure instead of being loose to be moved around during the drive. You don't want to terrify the puppy by letting the crate slide around while the puppy is inside it, sitting helplessly. This kind of jostling will teach your canine that cars are terrifying instead of making them feel safe.

First Night Frights

That first night is going to be incredibly scary to your little Pomeranian puppy. Away from mommy and any siblings, as well as the humans the puppy has come to know at the old home, it is understandable if the puppy is terrified. As understandable as this may be, there is only so much comfort you can give your new family member. Just like with a baby, the more you respond to cries and whimpering, the more you are teaching a puppy that negative behaviors will provide the desired results. You will need to be prepared for a balancing act to provide reassurance that things will be

Photo Courtesy of
DeQuita L Frost
Pomeranian Palace

CHAPTER 5 Bringing Home Your Pomeranian

all right while keeping your puppy from learning that crying gets your attention.

You should have a sleeping area established for the puppy prior to the arrival. It should include a bed, and probably a crate or pen. The entire area should be blocked off so that no one can get into it (and the puppy cannot get out) during the night. It should also be close to where people sleep so that the puppy does not feel abandoned.

Things like sounds may attract your puppy's attention, and those unfamiliar sounds can be scary. If you can minimize the number of noises, this could help make the first night a little less terrifying. These noises may not be as noticeable to you, but dogs have a much better sense of hearing.

> **HELPFUL TIP**
> **Puppy Night-lights**
>
> Night-lights for dogs can be a controversial topic. After all, dogs have better night vision than humans! Some puppies have a difficult time adjusting to sleeping in new places, however, and providing a night-light may help to reduce symptoms of anxiety. If you notice that your dog is exhibiting symptoms of anxiety at night, you might consider using a dim night-light to see if this provides some comfort. If you're considering a night-light to help prevent your pup from stumbling into anything in the dark, you may not need to worry. Dogs have good night vision and are quick to adapt to new surroundings. If you've provided a safe environment for your dog, you likely have little to worry about.

If you were able to get a blanket or pillow that smells like the mother, you will want to make sure this is in your puppy's space, particularly at night. The best way to get an item that smells familiar to the puppy is for you to send a blanket along that the breeder can place with the mother for a few days before the puppy comes home. The blanket can then also travel with the puppy in the car on the way to your place.

Your puppy is certainly going to make noises over the course of the night, and you cannot think of them as an inconvenience (no matter how tired you are). The puppy is sad and scared, so you will just need to endure it. Do not move the puppy away from you, even if the whimpering keeps you awake. Being moved away from people will only scare the puppy more, reinforcing the anxiety and fear of your home. Doing this on the first night will make the wrong impression, starting things off on the wrong footing. Over time, simply being close to you at night will be enough to reassure your puppy that everything will be all right.

Not getting much sleep should be something you expect during that first week or so (just like with an infant), but especially that first night. Make sure you don't have work or anything pressing the next day so that the lack

of sleep isn't too disruptive. Losing sleep is part of the deal of bringing a puppy into your home. Fortunately, it doesn't take as long to get a puppy acclimated as it takes with a human infant, so your normal schedule can resume more quickly.

You will need to learn to ignore the whining, but that will get easier over time so that the puppy doesn't learn to do this every night. If you give in, over time the whimpering, whining, and crying will get louder. Spare yourself the trouble later by teaching the puppy that it won't work.

Do not let your puppy into your bed that first night – or any other night until they are fully housetrained. Once a Pomeranian learns that the bed is accessible, you cannot train them not to hop on it. If they are not housetrained, you are going to need a new bed in the very near future.

The last thing that is going to cut into your sleep is the need for regular bathroom breaks. You can set up something in the puppy's space, or you can plan for trips outside every few hours (depending on how you plan to train your puppy). Whatever housetraining path you use, you are going to need to keep to a schedule even during the night to train your puppy where to use the bathroom. Puppies will need to go to the bathroom every two to three hours, and you will need to get up during the night to make sure they understand that they are to always go to the bathroom either outside or on the wee pad. If you let it go at night, you are going to have a difficult time training them that they cannot go in the house later.

First Vet Visit

This is going to be a difficult task because you may feel a bit like you are betraying your puppy (especially with the looks your puppy will give you during shots and the following visits to the vet). However, it is necessary to do this within the first day or two of your puppy's arrival. You need to establish a baseline for the puppy's health so that the vet can track progress and monitor the puppy to ensure everything is going well as your Pomeranian develops and ages. It also creates a rapport between your Pomeranian and the vet, which can help too. The initial assessment gives you more information about your puppy, as well as giving you a chance to ask the vet questions and get advice.

It is certain to be an emotional trip for your Pomeranian, although it could be exciting in the beginning. Wanting to explore and greet everyone and everything is going to be something that your puppy is very likely to want to do. Both people and other pets are likely to attract your puppy's attention. This is a chance for you to work on socializing the puppy, though you will need to be careful. Always ask the person if it is all right for your puppy to meet any other pet, and wait for approval before letting your puppy move forward with meeting other animals. Pets at the vet's office are very likely to not be feeling great, which means they may not be very affable. You don't want a grumpy older dog or a sick animal to nip, hurt, or scare your puppy. Nor do you want your puppy to be exposed to anything potentially dangerous while still going through the shots. You want the other animal to be happy about the meeting (though not too excited) so that it is a positive experience for your puppy.

Having a positive first experience with other animals can make the visit to see the vet less of a scary experience, and something that your Pomeranian can enjoy, at least a little. This can help your puppy feel more at ease during the visits.

Depending on what the vet does during the first visit, you may want to be prepared to comfort your puppy. It probably won't involve shots, but even without them, vets can be overwhelming and scary for puppies. The first vet visit really should not include shots as your puppy is a new arrival, and shots will make your puppy feel less than comfortable.

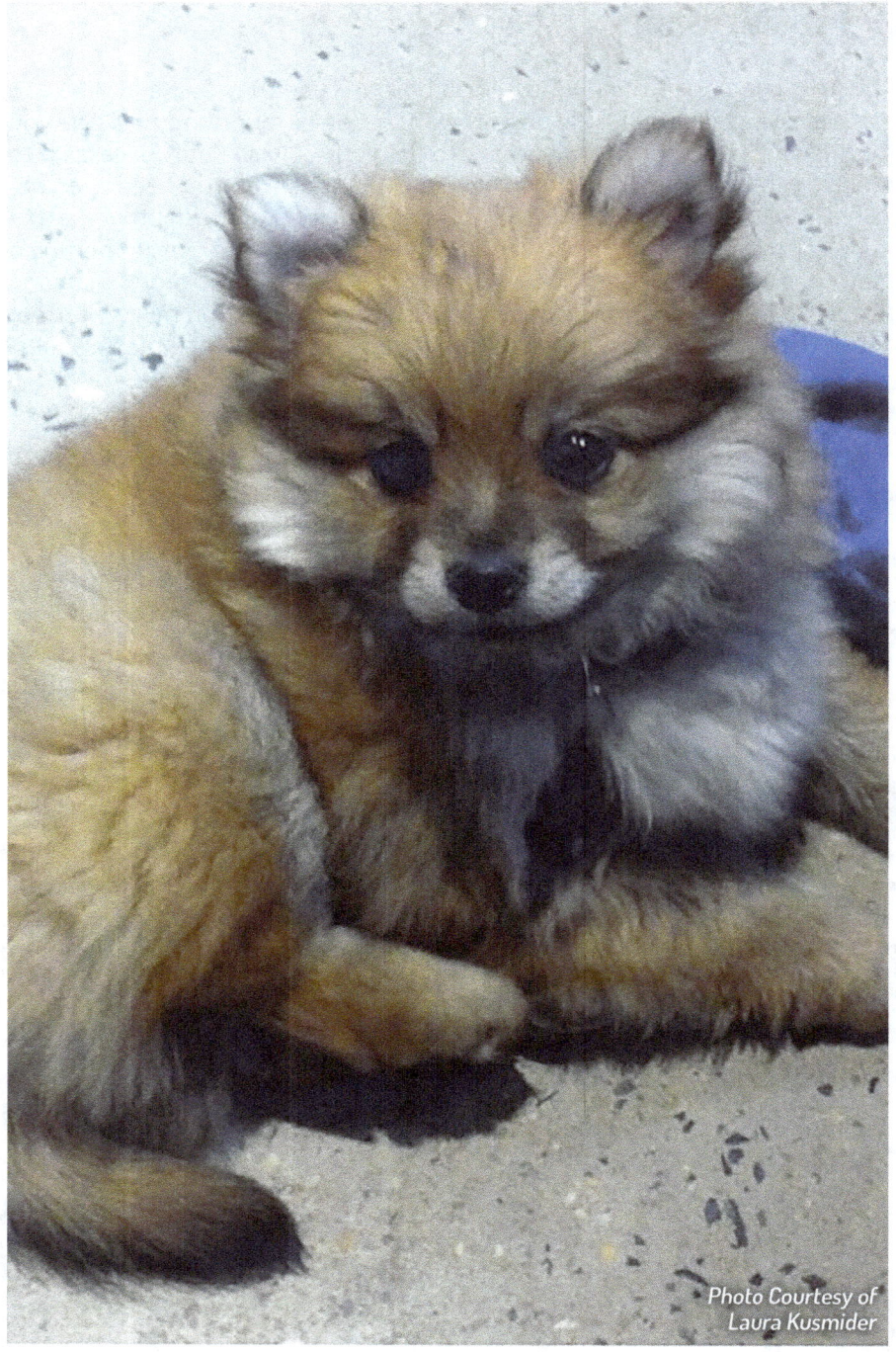

Photo Courtesy of Laura Kusmider

CHAPTER 5   Bringing Home Your Pomeranian

The Start Of Training

"They may do a lot of barking. Tell them 'No' or 'good dog' as a command and respond with a treat. Always use praise, they love praise."

Therese Perrien
Perrien's Pomeranians

As mentioned, training starts from the moment your Pomeranian becomes your responsibility, and that will be true for the entire life of your pooch. The first few weeks are going to be intense when it comes to training because you are establishing yourself as the alpha and trying to learn the best way to train your Pomeranian. It will be the foundation for all of the training, so this is when you need to start taking a firm and consistent approach, not later when your puppy is a bit older. This will be difficult, and firm isn't the same as mean. It will be an interesting training time for you as much as for puppy.

The focus during these first few weeks is to minimize undesirable behavior. You can start considering what kinds of training you would like for your puppy to have, but you should not be taking your puppy out to any classes or training during this first week. Most puppies have not had all of the necessary shots, and good trainers will not allow them in classes until the full first round of shots are complete.

CHAPTER 6.
The First Month

"Pomeranians are very loyal dogs, they will stick by their owners. They can teach owners about true companionship and what it means to love someone unconditionally."

Fatihah Mach
Lunar Poms

Once you finish that first week, you will have a fairly good idea of what your pup's personality is, and you will have a rough idea of what kind of routine will work with your puppy. You are probably feeling a bit tired as you have been sleeping a bit less than you need to, and because of the amount of effort needed to establish the foundation of training. One thing is certain, your life will be very different than it was before that first week.

Fortunately, this is where things start to gel and life will get easier. You have an idea of what kinds of tactics work best to motivate your Pomeranian. Praise probably is working pretty well since your puppy is starting to bond with you and will love that happy look on your face. Knowing this is going to make the rest of the month a lot easier to manage. By the time the month is out, you will almost certainly see some progress.

The biggest issue you will probably encounter over the coming weeks is how adorable your puppy is. It will be easy to feel that something is close enough, or that there will be time later to train. These are both understandable, but detrimental to your puppy's place in the pack and intellect. Don't be fooled by those puppy dog eyes – your Pomeranian can learn and will be much happier if you are firm (not mean) and consistent in your approach to training. Training should also be done daily, if only for short periods of time, to get your pup used to the idea of training. You should see some results of the training by the end of the month, although the results may not seem very big. Small steps must be taken to get your puppy to be the perfect companion

CHAPTER 6   The First Month

Photo Courtesy of Tanya Willard

Not Up To Full Strength – Don't Overdo It In The First Month

> *"When they are puppies, Poms are delicate and tiny, but brave and if you aren't holding them firmly they will jump off your lap, and could break their leg."*
>
> *Claudia Wallen*
> *Pearl Moon Poms*

Pomeranian puppies may seem like boundless furballs of energy, but they tire much faster than their adult counterparts. Their energy is limited, which means that you can tire them out quickly. This can be incredibly helpful in getting rid of all the energy, but you also have to be careful that you aren't pushing the training past the puppy's concentration threshold.

You won't be able to do nearly as much with your puppy over that first month because of their limited energy levels. Walks will be incredibly short. Tailor your activities to your puppy's current energy levels, mostly staying at home as much as possible so that your puppy can sleep once that energy is expended.

There will be walks on leashes, but that is still largely a learning experience. If you have a yard, that can also be a great place to play. Still, most of your trips will be within a block or two of home. Typically, these excursions will end with a nice puppy nap, meaning you won't be overly tired but will have time to do things you need to do without feeling like your puppy misses you. The puppy will still need to sleep in the designated puppy area because when that little pup wakes up, you may not be in the room. This is why it is important to pretty much stay home and not take your puppy out exploring in that first month. They simply don't have the energy and will feel more comfortable sleeping in the established space.

Don't worry – by the month's end, your puppy will have a lot more stamina so you can enjoy longer walks and short trips away from home if needed. You will need to start changing those exercise sessions to be longer so that your puppy can continue to build stamina and work on training a little further from home. Pomeranians will never really be the kind of dog to take on long walks or hikes, but at their best a couple of 30-minute walks a day will help keep your puppy healthy, and give you a bit more daily exercise.

CHAPTER 6 The First Month

Photo Courtesy of Debra Geist

For now, monitor your Pom's energy levels so that you aren't pushing for too long a walk or play session. Even if your Pomeranian can't handle a long walk, you still need to make sure that the puppy gets adequate activity every day. Remember, they are an intelligent breed, which means they will get in trouble when they get bored. Staying active will help them to not only be healthy, but keep them mentally stimulated so that they are less likely to get in trouble around the home. You will quickly realize just how sedentary you have been if you did not have a dog before because you will be on the move almost all of the time the puppy is awake.

Setting The Rules And Sticking To Them

> **HELPFUL TIP**
> **Swimming as Exercise**
>
> Swimming is an excellent, low-impact exercise for dogs. Most people don't think of Pomeranians when they think of dogs who like to swim, but many Pomeranians actually enjoy swimming! It's important to consider safety when determining if your Pomeranian will like swimming. Do not put your dog in deep water, a lake, or the ocean. Try a shallow pool or kiddie pool instead, and make sure to provide supervision for your dog's safety. If your Pomeranian is swimming in a chlorinated pool, make sure to wash your pup afterwards, as chlorine can dry out a dog's coat.

Pomeranians are notoriously headstrong, though they will be far less so when they are puppies. This is why it is essential for you to fight that urge to dote on them and let them get away with things when they are young. If you allow exceptions for the puppy, that puppy is going to grow into an adult that expects you to constantly allow exceptions. All puppies (regardless of breed) need a firm approach to training and the house rules, perhaps even more than adult dogs because they need a baseline of understanding. Never make exceptions in the early days to ensure the training sticks.

If you don't remain consistent, you are setting yourself and your Pom up for a lot of contention since it will be difficult to convince your dog that you are serious. You have already proved to your puppy that listening to you is optional. With the right look or action, the puppy can get you to lose focus, and will use this constantly in the future, and expect the same results. You will already be in the habit of giving in, making it that much harder to train both of you in the right way to behave.

Remember, they are stubborn, so training is important to get them to listen to you and to understand that you are in charge.

A firm, consistent approach is best for both of you. You want to have fun together, but that also means making sure your Pom knows that there are some things that are required, especially listening to you. Once your canine learns to listen to you, training your Pom to do tricks can be a enjoyable. It just takes some time to get there in the early days.

If you can manage to be firm and consistent over that first month, things could get a bit easier in the subsequent months. Keeping a level head and applying the rules without any exceptions paves the way for easier training. There will be a trust and respect that is built up from being a great trainer who keeps all of the lines clear, making the rest of your time with your Pom so much more enjoyable.

CHAPTER 6   The First Month

Photo Courtesy of
Cherie Disque

Treats And Rewards Vs. Punishments

Training and treats are so closely thought of together that it can be difficult to consider anything else as an effective means of training your dog. Second to treats, people think of punishment as a way of dissuading dogs from undesirable behavior. Although these have been the typical methods used in training, there are serious problems with both. Teaching a puppy proper behavior is a balancing act to make sure that you are firm, but not cruel, so you should provide rewards, but use something better than food.

Positive reinforcement can be an effective way to train Poms if you have established yourself as the pack leader. Food is an obvious choice, but you have to be very careful not to overfeed your puppy. You don't want the little pup to get accustomed to eating too much, especially as they become adults and no longer have a rapid metabolism. Starting with small treats is best, but you should quickly begin using praise and extra petting as the primary form of positive reinforcement. You could even add some extra playtime after a training session if your puppy does very well.

Photo Courtesy of Kat O'Brien

CHAPTER 6   The First Month

Having your puppy's respect is also essential for successful training. If your Pom respects you, it will be much easier for them to accept positive attention instead of treats because they know you are in charge.

You may occasionally need to resort to punishment, particularly if they nip or chew on furniture. However, you have to be careful not to train them to believe in things or actions that will make your life more difficult. Never use the crate as a place to punish your Pomeranian – it should be a safe haven when your puppy wants to be alone or sleep. It is not a jail and you should not treat it as one. You can use time out instead to get your point (and disappointment) across to the puppy. It should be somewhere that the puppy cannot interact with you, no matter how much the pup barks, whines, or whimpers, but you should still be visible to your puppy. You don't want to scare the puppy. The point is to let them know that you are still there but intentionally not interacting because of the puppy's actions. By denying them access to you without you disappearing, you are reminding them just why they need to behave.

Separation Anxiety

Pomeranians can get really attached to their people, which can lead to separation anxiety. This can be particularly true during the first month when your puppy is missing mommy and the first home. As prolific barkers who are not quite trained, puppies can literally bark for hours, which is really bad if your live in an apartment or with just walls separating you from your neighbors. The anxiety can also lead to destructive behaviors.

In the beginning, keep the puppy's time alone to a minimum. If you can work from home for the first month or two, or if you can constantly have a family member at home, this will help the puppy get acclimated. Alone time can involve being alone in the room. The sounds of people around the house will help your Pom understand that the separation is not permanent. After the first week or so, the alone time can involve you going out to get the mail, leaving the puppy inside alone for just a few minutes. You can then lengthen the amount of time over a few days until the puppy is alone for 30 minutes or so.

Here are some basic guidelines when you start to leave your puppy alone.
- Take the puppy out about 30 minutes before you leave.
- Tire the puppy out so that your leaving is not such a big deal.
- Place the puppy in the puppy area well ahead of when you go out to avoid associating the space with something bad happening.
- Don't give your puppy extra attention right before you leave because that reinforces the idea that you give attention before something bad happens.
- Avoid reprimanding your Pom for any behavior while you are away. This teaches them to be more stressed because it seems like you come home angry.

If your Pom exhibits signs of separation anxiety, there are several things you can do to help make the puppy comfortable during your absence.
- Chew toys can give your puppy something acceptable to gnaw on while you are away.
- A blanket or shirt that smells like you or other family members can help provide comfort too. Just make sure you don't give your puppy dirty clothing while you are away.

CHAPTER 6 The First Month

- Leave the area well lit, even if it is during the day. Should something happen and you get home later than intended, you don't want your Pomeranian to be in the dark.
- Turn on a stereo (classical music is best) or television (old-timey shows that don't have loud noises, like Mr. Ed or I Love Lucy) so that the home isn't completely quiet and unfamiliar noises are less obvious.

Since they are smart, it is not going to take your Pom long to notice the kind of behaviors that indicate you are leaving. Grabbing your keys, purse, wallet, and other indications will quickly become triggers that can make your Pom anxious. Don't make a big deal out of it. If you act normal, over time this will help your Pom to understand that your leaving is fine and that everything will be all right.

Training Areas To Start During The First Month

Training is covered in a later chapters, but there are several critical aspects that you will need to start during the first month:

- Housetraining
- Crate training
- Chewing
- Barking

You need to find out how much the breeder did in housetraining and other areas. The best trainers may even have puppies listening to one or two commands.

CHAPTER 7.
Housetraining

"Puppies will pee everywhere, it's important to pick a potty training tactic and start enforcing it. Keep your puppy close so you can continue to monitor their potty behavior to see if it's improving or not."

Fatihah Mach
Lunar Poms

While it's no one's favorite part of having a puppy, housetraining is an essential part of puppy planning. If you decide to adopt a puppy, you are going to have to housetrain him. With a stubborn pup like the Pomeranian, you may be in for quite the challenge too. Using a leash can be incredibly helpful in ensuring that your puppy learns when to go, but there will still be challenges as you work to establish the hierarchy and convince your puppy to listen to you. Remember, this is a type of training, so the system you use with other training will apply here. This is when you will need the most amount of patience with that firm and consistent training approach.

Two rules should be followed during this time.

1. Your puppy is not to be left free to roam the house when no one is around to monitor the puppy. Your Pom won't be pleased with the idea of being in a soiled crate, so that is a deterrent from using the bathroom when you are not around.

2. Your puppy should have constant, easy access to the locations where you plan to housetrain. If you cannot provide this, you will need to have frequent trips outside as your puppy learns where to do his business. This is the best way to train a puppy to go outside, and a leash can help you combine housetraining with leash training (although this could make it a little more difficult).

Start with a training plan, then make sure that you are as strict with yourself as you are with your puppy Or actually, be even more firm on yourself. You are the key to the puppy learning to go in the spots you want used for this particularly difficult aspect of training your companion. To make this plan work, you need to make some decisions so that you can best prepare for this difficult training.

CHAPTER 7 Housetraining

Inside Or Outside – Potty Training Options

Training a Pomeranian is very different from training most other breeds. There are risks to them that are only relevant to a few other very small breeds (like Chihuahuas), but their intellect creates unique challenges that are often associated with larger dogs. However, once a Pom understands to use the bathroom outside, you won't have to be as wary of them going inside as long as you keep a schedule and get them outside on that schedule.

If your breeder already started housetraining your dog, you don't have to think about it because you need to follow their schedule and methods. Your Pom is already accustomed to a particular method, and changing it will make your Pom more likely to either get confused or to believe that housetraining is optional.

Photo Courtesy of DeQuita L Frost Pomeranian Palace

Your Housetraining Options And Considerations

Of course, you are going to have to start housetraining inside, which is why you are going to need pee pads in the beginning. There should be one in the corner of the puppy space for the puppy to start using as the purpose of it becomes clear. Over time, training can change. Here are your options when it comes to housetraining your puppy:

- Pee pads – you should have several around the home for training
- Regular outings outside – set the schedule based on your puppy's sleeping and eating schedule
- Rewards – this can be treats in the beginning, but should quickly shift to praise

There are several factors that will influence how you begin training, particularly the weather outside. If the weather is too cold or hot, stick with training your puppy inside. They are not likely to focus if they are too uncomfortable. If they associate going to the bathroom with discomfort, they are going to be much more stubborn than if they are able to relieve themselves inside where it is more comfortable.

If you are able to start outdoor training, you should know that you are going to need to go out every two or three hours – including in the middle of the night. After a few weeks, you will be able to go out less frequently, but in the beginning the best way to housetrain is by going out a lot of times so that your puppy learns to keep all business outside. During the first few months, it is best to use a leash when you take the puppy out too. This not only keeps them safe, it allows you to help them learn to walk on a leash and keeps them from getting distracted.

CHAPTER 7   Housetraining

Setting A Schedule And Outdoor Restroom Location

Those early days are going to be difficult. You need to keep an eye on your puppy and have housetraining sessions after several key activities:

- After eating
- After waking up from sleeping or naps
- On a schedule (after it has been established)

"Always listen to your dog."

Margaret Mizushima, American author

Make sure you take your puppy outside or to a pee pad during these times because it is very likely that the little guy will need to go. This will make it a bit easier to train if you are telling your puppy to do something the Pomeranian wants to do.

Watch your Pomeranian for cues and to determine what activities make the little pup have to go. Start tailoring your schedule around your puppy's unique needs.

Puppies have small bladders and little control in the early days. If you have to train him to go inside, there needs to be a single designated space with a clean pee pad, and you need to stock up on the appropriate pads for the puppy to have somewhere to go that isn't the floor. The pads are better than newspaper and can absorb more. You will need to plan to transition as quickly as possible before the Pomeranian learns that going inside is acceptable – this will be incredibly difficult to retrain later if you let them go inside for too long, particularly as they realize that it is easier to go inside. The fact that you really cannot let them go out alone means you cannot have a doggy door with a Pom. This means that your dog is always going to rely on going to the restroom on your terms.

The designated restroom space can help make the experience easier. The Pomeranian will begin to associate that area of the yard for one purpose. When you get there, the expectation will be easier to understand faster than if you let the puppy sniff around and go anywhere in the yard. It also makes it a lot easier to clean up the yard as you won't have to hunt for where the puppy went – it's all in one place.

When out for walks is the perfect time to train your puppy to go. Between walks and the yard, your puppy will come to see the leash as a sign that it is time to relieve the bladder, which could become a Pavlovian response. Given that they are so smart, it won't take them long to understand the correlation either.

Key Words

All training should include key words, even housetraining. You and all members of the family should know what words to use when training your dog where to go to the bathroom, and you should all be using it consistently. If you have paired an adult with a child, the adult should be the one using the keyword during training.

It would be best to watch a few videos providing some hints and tips on training and the words that are often used. You have to be careful not to select words that you often use inside the home because you don't want to confuse your puppy. Selecting the right word is a lot trickier than you might think because you use some of the words in conversation more often than you might expect (particularly if you are potty training a child at the same time).

Positive Reinforcement – Rewarding Good Behavior

Positive reinforcement works quite well for Poms, even the puppies. If you can make healthy treats, that will make it a lot easier to use treats instead of changing to praise as quickly. You can also use Cheerios because they are small and don't add a lot of calories to your pup's diet.

Take a few pieces of kibble with you when you are teaching your puppy where to go both inside and outside. Learning that you are the one in charge will help teach the Pom to look to you for cues and instructions. They may try to push you a bit as their stubbornness begins to show, or to convince you that it's okay to let things slide because they want to enjoy time with you – not be forced to do something. You have to work through this and reinforce the need for them to go when on the schedule.

While you are being firm and consistent, when your puppy does the right thing you have to lavish the little pup with praise. This is just as effective because Poms love to see their people happy. They want to hear that they are good, and if you give them an extra treat or kibble, this will put them over the moon. Over time, you will begin to transition from treats to praise, which is better for both your Pom's health and your budget.

If you gently lead your puppy to the area on a leash, it will become obvious over time that your Pomeranian should go there to use the bathroom. When you move away from treats, your Pom will start to associate using the bathroom with a bit of extra playtime and praise.

CHAPTER 7   Housetraining

    Ultimately, Poms are notoriously difficult to housetrain. If your breeder already started the training, some of the worst of it has already been taken care of it for you. This will make training easier. However, Pomeranians are incredibly unique, which means that you have to tailor the training to your puppy. The best place to look for tips and tricks to help you with this difficult task is on Pomeranian HQ. They have a lengthy page that covers many different scenarios and problems you may encounter, as well as the solutions. Don't forget, if you found a great breeder, you can always call them and ask for solutions. Odds are good they have been through it themselves and they can provide you with guidance to help you through the trials and tribulations of housetraining an intelligent, stubborn dog that isn't interested in doing something so basic on someone else's terms.

    On the plus side, nearly all other training is going to seem easy by comparison.

CHAPTER 8.
Socialization And Experience

Photo Courtesy of Jess Smith

Pomeranians can be incredibly gregarious when they want to be, and their boldness and curiosity will mean they won't be afraid to leave home. With proper socialization, they won't feel a need to be aggressive when faced with bigger dogs (which is nearly every other dog given how tiny Poms are). To make sure your Pom is happy to encounter other people and dogs, you need to make sure you plan for socializations as soon as it is safe to do so. Your puppy will need to have all of the necessary vaccinations before being exposed to other dogs, but that happens fairly early in your puppy's life. Once those vaccinations are out of the way, you should start socializing your puppy.

Since they aren't afraid, socialization should be fairly easy as long as you start early. This means you have to plan for it even before your puppy arrives. Without planning and a controlled environment, socialization can go very wrong, very quickly. If you keep things simple and under control, your Pomeranian will learn to relax and enjoy the company of other people and dogs.

Socialization with your current dogs is slightly different, and is covered in the next chapter. Even if you have dogs, you are going to need to socialize your new Pom with other dogs because your current dogs are part of their pack. That means that they don't count toward socializing with the outside world.

CHAPTER 8 Socialization And Experience

Photo Courtesy of Cassie Revett

Photo Courtesy of Sandra Reigart

The Importance Of Socialization

It is always important to socialize dogs, but even more so with small dogs. People are inclined to be overprotective and cautious with small dogs and puppies, and this can lead to serious problems later. With Pomeranians being so small, somewhat fragile, and absolutely adorable, there is an inclination to be overprotective. You will need to let your puppy say hello, but there are some safe ways to do that.

The benefit of early socialization is that it can make things that much more enjoyable for everyone involved, no matter what the situation is. A socialized dog will approach the world from a much better place than a dog that is not socialized. All other rules still apply during socialization, so keep that in mind while you help your dog meet new friends.

CHAPTER 8   Socialization And Experience

If you do not properly socialize your Pomeranian, no amount of training is going to help your dog better interact with other animals and humans. You will probably want to be protective, but treating your Pomeranian like a doll or an infant could cause the development of small dog syndrome. They need to be allowed to learn how to interact with others so that they aren't always terrified or upset

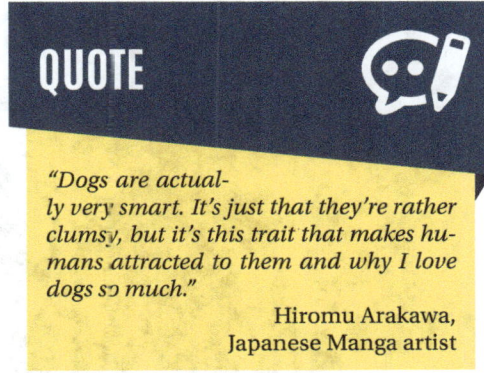

QUOTE

"Dogs are actually very smart. It's just that they're rather clumsy, but it's this trait that makes humans attracted to them and why I love dogs so much."

Hiromu Arakawa,
Japanese Manga artist

with you when there are other people or dogs around them. It isn't healthy for your Pomeranian to always be anxious or nervous around others, especially when you can easily avoid it. Make time to socialize your puppy to make his life enjoyable and so that he is as happy to meet new people and dogs as you and your family are.

Socialization teaches your puppy to enjoy the world around them instead of to feel a need to prove themselves. Poms already have a tendency to be mistrustful of strangers, and this will be exacerbated if you do not make the time to socialize them when they are young. The most common problems with Pomeranians is their barking and potential aggressive behavior when they aren't socialized. This can get very frustrating as they get older, so you do not want to encourage this kind of behavior when they are puppies, even if they are cute.

Photo Courtesy of Clarissa Gerber

Properly Greeting New People

It can be a lot of fun, so it isn't something most people avoid. (Who doesn't love meeting and playing with a lovable little dog?) The difficult part is finding the time to do it often enough to reinforce the positive behaviors and teach the puppy that the world is a fun place to live in.

Greeting new people is usually a pretty easy task outside of the home, but it can be a bit tricky when you are at home. Training your Pom how to treat visitors may take a little longer because he will very excited and will want to be the center of attention. In the end, it is worth the effort as your Pom becomes an enjoyable companion for you and anyone who visits.

Behavior Around Other Dogs

Pomeranians are incredibly agreeable dogs. They do not need to be the alpha dog, but they can believe that things should always be fun and exciting . If you have an older dog, most Pomeranians will be able to peacefully work out who is alpha and who isn't without too many problems. Since Pomeranians hate to be alone, it is probably better to have another dog if you are absent from the home for several hours every day.

By inviting over friends and family who have well behaved and friendly dogs of all sizes, you can make socialization much easier in the early days. Having people stop by who know how to interact with puppies can help your little Pom start to understand when visitors are to be welcomed and when to bark at a stranger at the door.

CHAPTER 9.
Living With Other Dogs

Pomeranians are incredibly loyal and they love their families, including other dogs in the family. However, it can take time to help them feel comfortable in their new surroundings. If you bring a puppy into your home, it will be a bit easier to help them understand that your dogs are safe to be around. Older Poms may or may not have problems with other dogs, though they do not yet consider your home their home quite yet. This can make it easier to introduce the new Pomeranian into their new home.

Introducing Your New Puppy

When it comes to meeting the puppy, this should be in neutral territory away from your home. Select a park or other area where your dog will not feel territorial and plan to introduce your dog to the puppy there. This gives them the opportunity to meet and get to know each other before entering the home together.

When you go to introduce your dog and puppy, make sure you have at least one other adult with you. It is best to have the whole family if possible, but having at least one other adult means that there is someone to manage each canine. If you have more than one dog, then you should have one adult per dog. This will make it easier to keep everyone under control. Even the best dogs can get overly excited about meeting a puppy. One of the people who needs to be there is the person who is in charge in the home (or people if you have more than one person in charge). This helps establish the pack hierarchy.

STORY
Boo and Buddy

Boo was a Pomeranian and the self-proclaimed "world's cutest dog." Boo had millions of followers on Facebook and appeared on Good Morning America on several occasions. In 2019, Boo passed away at the age of seven, two years after his companion Buddy passed away. After Buddy's death, Boo had begun to show signs of heart problems, leading the family to believe that Boo died of a broken heart once Buddy was no longer by his side.

CHAPTER 9   Living With Other Dogs

Photo Courtesy of Cassie Revett

The introductory time could take a while, depending on the personality of your dog. The friendlier and more accepting your dog is of the puppy, the easier it will be to incorporate your new puppy into the home. For some dogs a week is enough for them to start feeling comfortable together. For other dogs, it could take a couple of months before they are fully accepting of the new puppy. Since this is a completely new dynamic in your household, your current dog may not be pleased with you bringing a little bundle of energy into his daily life. This is enough to make anyone unhappy, but especially a dog that has grown accustomed to a certain lifestyle. The older your dog is, the more likely it is that a puppy will be an unwelcome addition. With their abilities limited, older dogs can get cranky around puppies that don't understand the rules or don't seem to know when enough is enough. The goal is to make your puppy feel welcome and safe, while letting your dog know that your love is just as strong as ever.

Once your new family member and the rest of the canine pack start to get acquainted and feel comfortable with each other, you can head home. As they enter the home, they will have a bit more familiarity with each other, making your current dogs feel more comfortable with the new addition to the family.

Photo Courtesy of Kassie Lamontagne

CHAPTER 9 Living With Other Dogs

Establishing The New Norm

This sense of familiarity established during the first meeting does not mean that the dogs will have bonded, so there may be some tension, especially early on. This is why it is important to keep them separated in the home, particularly when you are away. The puppy should be in the designated area, and it will be easier for your puppy to relax and start to get familiar with the new environment there. Since you set the special area up prior to your puppy's arrival, it will be much easier to start getting your puppy acclimated to his area.

Make sure that none of your other dog's stuff ends up in the puppy's area. This can be seen by your dog as a threat to his or her place in the pack and will generate unnecessary tension between your dog and the new puppy. The puppy will probably chew on anything and everything in the puppy's area, including things that belong to your other dog. At this stage, possessions don't mean anything to your little Pomeranian. Your dog, on the other hand, will see this as a challenge, likely resulting in negative behavior. This will be true when your puppy is out of the puppy area too. Make sure that all of your dog's stuff is out of the puppy's reach at all times. Before taking the puppy out of the designated area, make sure to do a bit of cleanup and store the dog's toys in a safe place.

Mealtime is another potential problem, so your puppy should be eating in a different location, at least in the beginning. Food tends to be the source of most dog fights and unnecessary tension. As your puppy gets older, you can start to feed your Pomeranian with your other dogs, but keep them separated.

Your current dog probably isn't going to be happy about sharing you with the puppy either. Be prepared to make sure your dog knows you still care about him or her after the puppy arrives because your dog is going to be pretty uncertain because of the new addition. Schedule one-on-one time with your dog, including longer walks, extra training, or general play. This will let your dog know that the puppy is not a replacement. You should start keeping a schedule with your dog so that you don't change the amount of time you spend together after the puppy arrives. It also means you will need to be just as firm and consistent with your puppy as you are with your dog. If you are more lenient with your puppy than with your dog, this will create tension between your dog and the puppy.

There are a number of benefits to having a dog in the home that already knows the rules. The biggest is that your dog will also start scolding your puppy for misbehavior. Since your dog isn't likely to be swayed

by how cute the puppy is, your dog will have a much more objective approach to training. Of course, your dog cannot be the primary trainer, but it is nice to have someone helping reinforce the rules and showing the puppy how things are done. Having a dog to set an example helps the puppy better understand where he or she is in the pack while learning what behaviors are unacceptable. As long as your dog is gentle with the new member of the family, it is all right to let your well-behaved dog scold and reprimand your puppy – just make sure there isn't too much aggression or roughness to the behavior correction. Having your own canine babysitter also helps establish a better relationship between the canines.

Should your dog opt out of this role, that isn't a problem either. There is no need to force a role on your current dogs because their behavior will be enough to show the puppy how to behave. It is best to let your dog decide what kind of relationship he wants to have with the puppy.

Intelligent dogs can pick up things incredibly fast, so they can quickly grasp a situation, which may or may not work in your favor. Puppies don't have the experience to make these kinds of judgments or assessments. What they do have is an understanding that things are changing, which can make them understandably apprehensive. They are going to need reassur-

CHAPTER 9   Living With Other Dogs

ance and attention as they get situated. This could cause contention with your current canine companions – this is why it is essential to make sure you make time for your current dogs every day.

Once your Pom accepts your other dogs (and vice versa), your Pom will be as protective of your dogs as he is of you. This can be wonderfully entertaining, particularly if you have bigger dogs. It is nearly certain that your Pom is going to be the most outgoing of the bunch, and that can lead to some very interesting encounters. Being smart, your Pomeranian will be able to know when to step up for your dogs, but with socialization, that will not be often, making your trips outside enjoyable.

Biting, Fighting, And Puppy Anger Management With Multiple Pom Puppies

Only the brave puppy parents adopt more than one puppy at a time, and this is true even with dogs like the Pomeranian. It is at least twice as much work and you will have to split your attention between two or more puppies at the same time. If you want to raise more than one Pomeranian puppy at once, you are in for a real challenge. They are going to want to please you and spend time with you, but they are also likely to feel something similar for each other. They have the same energy level and desire to learn, which means that their misbehaviors can feed off each other. It will take a lot more energy and work to make sure they behave the way you want them to act.

Be prepared to lose your personal life, particularly your social life, if you have more than one puppy at a time. Taking care of those little puppies is going to be like two full-time jobs. It is necessary to put a lot of work into training your puppies so that your home isn't destroyed twice as fast.

First, you must spend time with them both, together and separately. This does mean spending twice as much time with the puppies, making sure they get along well, learn at an even pace, and still get to have designated time with you. Each puppy will have its own strengths and weaknesses, and you need to learn what those are for each one, as well as learning how well the puppies work together. If they both behave during alone time with you, but tend to misbehave or fail to listen when they are together, you will need to adjust your approach to make sure they both understand the rules. This is a real challenge, especially if they whine when you are playing with one of them and not the other (which is very likely with Pomeranians).

You can always have someone else play or train with one puppy while you do the same with the other, then switch puppies. This builds bonds while letting the puppies know that they both have to listen to you and your training partner. Both puppies will also be happily occupied, so they won't be whimpering or feeling lonely while you are playing with the other puppy.

Photo Courtesy of Kat O'Brien

There may be some fighting between the puppies, and this is likely to start when they are between three and six months of age. They don't tend to be as aggressive as other dogs, but it is still almost certain that there will be minor fights. This is fine as long as they are not too aggressive. Likely it won't be because Pomeranians are less concerned with where they are in the hierarchy than in being with their people. As long as they understand the rules and abide by them, fighting should not be a significant problem with your puppies.

CHAPTER 9   Living With Other Dogs

During training, you will need to minimize distractions, both for your puppy and yourself. This is why serious training should be done one-on-one more often than together. Puppies are always watching and learning, especially when you have a dog that is as enamored with you as the Pomeranian tends to be. If you do not properly train them, it will be your fault when they become difficult adults that won't listen to you. Be consistent and focused during training to avoid the worst behavior problems.

CHAPTER 10.
Training Your Pomeranian Puppy

Because your Pomeranian is a quick learner and an intelligent dog, you would think that training your puppy would be quick and easy. The problem with all smart dogs is that they tend to be more independent and want to have things their way. Pomeranians are notoriously stubborn, which can mean training can be much harder and more frustrating than with other dogs.

Knowing that you need to take a different approach can be incredibly helpful when it comes to training a smarter dog. You can prepare for the unique challenges. More importantly, you can anticipate that your dog understands and knows that you need to keep your patience up as you focus on training your dog to listen instead of trying to teach your dog what you mean.

Working with a smart, energetic puppy can be tiring. By making sure to follow through with a few actions, you will find that your Pomeranian will pick up on the training much quicker. Keep in mind that training your puppy is a long-term commitment. Even if your Pomeranian isn't rebellious, the puppy probably just wants to have fun. Your puppy won't want to anger you, but gentle begging and puppy eyes can be very effective against all but the most determined parent, and Pomeranians will learn that, particularly if you give in during a training session.

Photo Courtesy of Shania Huge

CHAPTER 10   Training Your Pomeranian Puppy

Firm And Consistent

There are many times in training where you will feel something is close enough. This is never a good idea with intelligent dogs. They study their people and figure out ways to get what they want with as little work as possible. Wanting to please you will still motivate a Pomeranian, but if you are willing to give an inch, they will take it and then see how much further you can be pushed. Exceptions and leniency are seen by your puppy as having some control over the situation, and that is not something you want them to learn when they are young. It just makes it that much harder to make them take you seriously later.

Keeping a consistent and firm approach during training will make life far easier for you and your puppy. Even if you are tired at the end of a long day at work, you have to enforce the rules. No matter how cute or friendly your puppy is being, you must make sure that all of the rules you have been teaching remain firmly in place. If you don't feel up to it, have a family member do the training. If you don't have anyone to help you, you can change up the training a bit to make it more enjoyable. It is fine to change things up if you are having a rough time, as long as you remain consistent. Interacting with your Pomeranian can make for a much more enjoyable experience, and can even cheer you up. Consistency and firmness do not mean that you have to do the same thing all of the time. You just need to make sure that your puppy understands that you are in charge and there is no negotiating on that. This will keep your puppy on the right track to being a great companion instead of a little dictator.

Gain Respect Early

Being firm and consistent in your approach to training will start gaining you respect from your little canine early in your relationship. This is something you will need to keep building over time. Without respect, your Pomeranian is going to think you don't mean what you say, and will start to try to get its own way. As long as you are firm and consistent, respect should be a natural part of the bond. That does mean that you cannot multi-task while you are training your puppy, or even just playing with your puppy. The Pomeranian wants your full attention and will find a way to get it, even if it means breaking the rules to get your attention.

Positive reinforcement is the best way to gain respect, particularly if you use positive interaction. Playing and training your puppy every day helps build a healthy, positive relationship that will teach your puppy where he or she fits into the pack. Your puppy learns that it is part of the family, but that you are the one in charge.

Operant Conditioning Basics

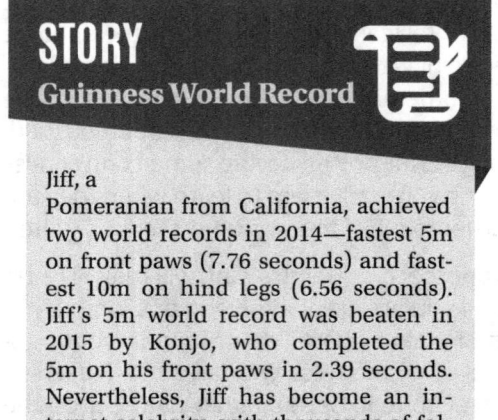

STORY — Guinness World Record

Jiff, a Pomeranian from California, achieved two world records in 2014—fastest 5m on front paws (7.76 seconds) and fastest 10m on hind legs (6.56 seconds). Jiff's 5m world record was beaten in 2015 by Konjo, who completed the 5m on his front paws in 2.39 seconds. Nevertheless, Jiff has become an internet celebrity, with thousands of followers on social networking sites such as Facebook, Instagram, Twitter, and YouTube. He also appeared in the Katy Perry music video for "Dark Horse."

Operant conditioning is the scientific term for actions and consequences. What you have to do is provide your Pomeranian puppy with the right consequences for each behavior.

The best way to use operant conditioning is through positive reinforcement, particularly since the Pomeranian is so attached to people. This type of training is more effective with working dogs and dogs that have a long history with people because they want to please their people. They want to work with you and fulfill their tasks. Knowing that they are doing something right does a lot more to encourage their behavior than knowing when they do something wrong. With so much energy, they will be able to keep trying until they get it right.

There are two types of reinforcements for operant conditioning:
- Primary reinforcements
- Secondary reinforcements

You will use both during your Pomeranian training.

Primary Reinforcements

A primary reinforcement gives your dog something that it needs to survive, like food or social interaction. Both of these can be effective for Pomeranians – they love spending time with you and may be happy to have treats. That is exactly what makes treats so effective during training.

Initially, you will rely on primary reinforcements since you do not have to teach your Pom to enjoy them. However, you have to keep a balance. Mealtime and playtime should never be denied to your puppy, no matter how poorly the puppy performs. These things are essential to living, and

CHAPTER 10 Training Your Pomeranian Puppy

you will have to give them the essentials – that is not negotiable. It is things like treats and extra playtime that you use to reinforce good behavior.

Err on providing too much attention and affection over too many treats. Because of their small stature, Pomeranian need to keep a well-balanced diet to be healthy. If you rely on treats instead of attention, you are setting yourself and your pup up for serious health problems later.

Secondary Reinforcements

You used repetition to get good at your hobbies, sports, and other physical activities – this is secondary reinforcement. Without a doubt, Pavlov's experiment with dogs is the most recognizable example of secondary reinforcement. Using the bell, Pavlov taught the test dogs that when the bell rang it meant it was time to eat. The dogs began to associate the ringing of a bell to mealtime. They were conditioned to associate something with a primary reinforcement. You can see this in your home when you use a can opener. If you have any cats or dogs, they probably come running as soon as the can opener starts going.

Photo Courtesy of Tanya Willard

Secondary reinforcements work because your Pomeranian will associate the trigger with something that is required. This makes your puppy more likely to do as you tell it to do. Dogs that are taught to sit using a treat only will automatically react by sitting down when you have a treat in your hand. They won't even wait for you to tell them to sit. They know that sitting means more food, so they automatically do it once you make that association. Of course, this is not the proper training because they need to learn to sit when you say sit, and not when you have a treat. That is the real challenge.

Fortunately, it is relatively easy to train Pomeranian puppies with the right trigger because they are both intelligent and eager to please. While they may enjoy food, you can show them that the trigger is the word, not the food. They will get it much faster than many other dog breeds.

You can also use toys and attention as a way of getting your Pomeranian to do the right thing. If you have a regular schedule and you are willing to change it a little to give your puppy a little extra attention for doing something right, that will be just as effective as a treat because they love attention. You can take the pup on an extra walk, spend a little more time playing with a favorite toy, or take some time to cuddle with the puppy.

Sometimes punishment is required too, but you need to be very careful about how you do it. Trying to punish a Pomeranian can be tricky, but denying your Pomeranian attention can work very well. Simply put your puppy in a penned off area where the Pomeranian can see you but cannot interact

Photo Courtesy of Stacey Papo

CHAPTER 10 Training Your Pomeranian Puppy

with you. The little guy will whine and whimper to let you know that he or she wants out. Don't give in because this is the punishment. Just ignore your puppy to teach the lesson about proper behavior.

Punishments must happen right after the event. If your Pomeranian chews something up and you don't find out for several hours, it is too late to punish the puppy. The same is true for rewards. To reinforce behavior, the reward or punishment must be almost immediate. When you praise or punish your puppy, make sure you keep eye contact. You can also take the puppy by the scruff of the neck to ensure that you keep eye contact. You won't need to do that when you are praising your pooch because he or she will automatically keep eye contact. Poms can be absolutely driven by hearing your praise.

Why Food Is A Bad Reinforcement Tool

Pomeranians are among the smallest canines in the world, making food a very dangerous incentive to rely on when training them. They really cannot handle a lot of additional weight, so you have to find other incentives that work better. Use treats sparingly.

Another reason to use treats sparingly is because you don't want your puppy to respond to you primarily when you have food. If your Pomeranian associates training with treats, you may have a difficult time training your Pom to listen to you without them.

Treats can be used in the early stages when your puppy's metabolism is high and has not been conditioned to respond to secondary reinforcements. This will give you something to help your puppy learn to focus as you train the puppy to understand other incentives. It should not take too long before you can start transitioning away from treats as a reinforcement tool. Treats are also the best way of training certain types of behavior, such as rolling over. Your puppy will automatically follow the treat, making it easy to understand what you mean.

Treats are also best for the beginning commands (sit, stay, and leave it). Your dog does not understand words yet, and will quickly make the connection between what you are saying and why the treat is being offered. Leave it is very difficult to teach without treats because there is no incentive to drop something if your puppy really wants the object already in his or her mouth. Treats are something that will make the puppy drop whatever is in the puppy's mouth as the attention and desire focuses on food.

Small Steps To Success

The first few weeks, or maybe even the first couple of months, are a time with a very steep learning curve. Your puppy is not going to understand what you are doing in the beginning as you try to convince your little Pom to use the bathroom outside. The best way to train the puppy is to realize that you need to start slow – don't begin with expectations that your puppy will be housetrained in a week (that won't happen). Your puppy must learn the daily routine (which you will be doing at the same time). Once the schedule and environment are less exciting, your Pom will have an easier time focusing during training sessions.

Training should begin from day 1. Even through your puppy is just getting to know the environment, you need to start putting some of the rules in place. As your puppy gets familiar with you and the environment, you can teach the Pomeranian about its area and that the crate is for sleeping. Learning to go into the crate on command has some obvious benefits, particularly if you leave home every day. This is when you start using treats to train the puppy to go into the crate and do other basic activities.

Starting from day 1 does not mean trying to do everything – you must start small. Give treats for little things that your puppy might do anyway, like explore the crate. Once your Pomeranian starts to understand the reward system, training will start to get easier.

Basic Behavior Training

The next chapter covers basic command training, but it is different than training your Pom of different types of behavior. Soon after your puppy arrives, you need to start training out the bad behaviors, and that is not restricted to just training sessions. It is something you need to constantly teach your puppy over the course of the day.

Chewing And Nipping

This one is going to be very important if your Pom has separation anxiety, but it is good to train your pup even if the little guy seems fine with you leaving. Chewing and nipping are definitely behaviors you want to stop as soon as possible.

- Say no in a strong, confident voice whenever your Pom starts chewing on anything that is not a toy or food or nips at you, another person, or another pet.

CHAPTER 10   Training Your Pomeranian Puppy

- Provide chew toys.
- Keep the Pom in the puppy pen until they don't chew on furniture and items in their reach.
- Get some puzzle toys to keep your Pom's brain engaged (some chew out of boredom).

Crate Training

Your Pom's crate needs to be comfortable. Time in the crate is not meant to be a punishment, so you want your puppy to be comfortable in the crate. It should also be a part of their puppy area, with their bed. This gives them a safe space.

Crate training can help with housetraining as well. Poms do not want to use the bathroom near their home – they don't want to soil their bedding. Having a pee pad in their puppy area but as far from the crate as possible will help to make the point that it is to be used for bladder relief.

Barking

Easily one of the most frustrating potential problems with Pomeranians, this is what you really have to plan to train out of your puppy (or dog). There are many ways to train your dog, but they all involve being patient. Yelling at your dog to teach it not to bark is the worst possible thing you could do.

It is basically doing exactly the same thing back at them, which will reinforce barking, not diminish the action.

As the breeder what their recommendation is. If they don't have any specifics, there are several sites that you can use and tailor your method to your Pom's triggers:

- Pomeranian HQ
- Pommy Mommy
- Wag
- Pet Pom

Why You May Want To Plan To Have A Trainer

Pomeranians are stubborn, and if you haven't dealt with a smarter dog, if you haven't trained a puppy or a dog, or if you don't have much patience, then you really should consider using a trainer. Even if you do have experience, it may be helpful in the beginning to have someone to help you. If you go online, virtually every site recommends that you try to do it yourself or that you transfer to training your Pom on your own as quickly as possible. This is largely because they are loyal to their people and are far less likely to be obedient with an outside. Since you have been training them since they arrived, you have a much better chance of training. Still, there will be times when having someone to help assist you can give you some emotional support to keep going.

Pomeranians are a particularly tricky dog to train because they are more intelligent than most other small dogs. Because of how adorable they are, it can be difficult to remain consistent or to know exactly when they are not doing something because they don't want to and when they aren't doing it because they don't understand. It is as much about knowing why your Pom isn't listening as it is to training them. Trainers can help you identify what you need to do in those early situations when you are still learning about your dog's personality.

Ultimately, you want your Pomeranian to enjoy training. Depending on your personality and experience, it may be best to have a trainer who can help train you while training your puppy. Classes can also be beneficial because it gives you a chance to socialize your dog before and after the class. Decide if you want your Pom trained as an individual or as part of a class.

Many classes are offered by local pet shops or vets, creating a more friendly environment. You can start with one of the Pomeranian organizations to see if they have any classes to recommend in your area. If that fails,

CHAPTER 10 Training Your Pomeranian Puppy

ask your vet to recommend classes or trainers. They often know trainers or can at least point you in the right direction.

The following are the types of training that you can consider:
- Obedience
- Basic commands
- People interaction
- Behavior modification
- Obstacle courses

Review the potential trainers' certifications and experiences. Looking at online reviews can help you determine if they have successfully trained other dogs. You should also find out if they have experience training Pomeranians. You want to verify that the trainer has several different methods that they use because a method that works for one dog isn't guaranteed to work for another. The training should be adjusted to work for your dog; otherwise, you are putting your Pomeranian at a disadvantage.

You want a trainer who will help you train while training your Pom. Classes are advised largely because the trainer is providing instruction to the people, then helps the pet parents to get better responses. Since you need to become the trainer as soon as possible, you definitely don't want the trainer to be doing all of the work. Pay attention to how they treat their students in the class too. If they are condescending or cruel, then you will not want to continue the classes.

Just like with your breeder, you want your trainer to be available outside of the class in case you are having problems with your Pomeranian. Don't waste their time, saving up questions that don't need an immediate answer for the class.

You are going to have to learn how to train a dog because eventually you will not have a trainer to help you. Dogs have to know that you are the one who is the alpha of the pack, and that means knowing how to be firm and consistent.

CHAPTER 11.
Basic Commands

Pomeranians are not always easy to train. Knowing this going in, you can take the right mental approach to training. It is entirely too easy to think that allowing those adorable little dogs to get away with something once or twice is fine, but it really isn't. Being successful in your training really requires a firm and consistent approach from the moment your Pom enters your care. This is how you gain their respect and help them understand the family hierarchy.

Why Size And Personality Make Them Ideal Companions

Photo Courtesy of Sherri J Osterland

Training is something that is a lot of fun with a Pomeranian. They are incredibly intelligent, and training them makes them even more fun to spend time with. When properly trained they can be one of the best companions you will ever have because they can travel with you anywhere you go. If a Pom is well trained, the people around you will also enjoy having the dog around too because the Poms are famous for their fun and energy. They tend to love everyone and want to play. Since they can go with you virtually anywhere, training will quickly pay off as you and your best friend share some of the most memorable lessons. If your Pom is not trained, it will be much harder to take your canine places as your Pom will be wary of strangers and may bark far more than is comfortable for anyone around him.

CHAPTER 11   Basic Commands

Photo Courtesy of Kassie Lamontagne

Picking The Right Reward

One of the most interesting aspects of having a Pom is determining the right reward. You want to keep the treats to a minimum but that should be fine with a Pom since there are so many other things that can motivate them. Treats may be a good starting point, but you will need to quickly switch to something that is a secondary reinforcer. Praise, additional playtime, and extra petting are all fantastic rewards for Pom pets since they care about how you feel and your reaction to them. Plopping down to watch a movie and letting the puppy sit with you will be a great reward after an intense training session. Not only did your puppy learn, but you both now get to relax and enjoy just chilling together.

If you begin to gain the respect of your Pom, that can be used to help train your dog. At the end of each session, give your puppy extra attention or a nice walk to demonstrate how pleased you are with the progress that has been made.

Successful Training

> *Some men can be good 'horse whisperers,' and many dogs can be wonderful 'man whisperers.'"*
> Erik Pevernagie, Belgian painter

Training is about learning the commands. If your Pom learns to respond only to the rewards (such as the dog that sits as soon as you have a treat in your hand), the training was not successful.

Gaining the respect of your dog is generally the key in being a successful trainer, but with a Pom it also means dedicated attention – you have all of the puppy's attention during a training session. As you and your Pom work together, your dog will come to respect you (so long as you remain consistent and firm). Do not expect respect in the early days of training because your puppy does not have the understanding or relationship required to be able to understand. Fortunately, their intelligence will start to show early on, making it easy to see when they are starting to respond to you instead of just the reward. This is the time when you can start switching to rewards that are fun instead of those that center around treats and food.

Even in the beginning, you need to make handling and petting a part of the reward. Although your dog does not quite understand it for what it is, your Pom will begin to understand that treats and petting are both types of rewards. This will make it easier to switch from treats to a more attention-based reward system. Associating handling and petting as being enjoyable will also encourage your puppy to look at play time as a great reward. No matter how much they love to eat, being entertained and playing with you will be a welcome reward since it means the puppy is not alone or bored.

CHAPTER 11 Basic Commands

Basic Commands

For the Pomeranian, there are five basic commands that you must teach them, and ones that you will probably want to start training your puppy to understand. These commands are the basis for a happy and enjoyable relationship as your Pom learns how to behave. By the time your puppy learns the five commands, the purpose of training will be clear to your Pom. That will make it much easier to train them on the more complex concepts.

You should train the puppy in the order of the list as well. Sit is a basic command, and something all dogs including your Pom already do. Teaching leave it and how to bark less are both difficult and fight the instincts and desires of your Pom pooch. These two commands are going to take longer to learn than the other commands, so you want to have the necessary tools already in place to increase your odds of success.

Here are some basic guidelines to follow during training.
- Everyone in the home should be a part of the Pom training because the Pom needs to learn to listen to everyone in the household, and not just one or two people.
- To get started, select an area where you and your puppy have no distractions, including noise. Leave your phone and other devices out of range so that you keep your attention on the puppy.
- Stay happy and excited about the training. Your puppy will pick up on your enthusiasm, and will focus better because of it.
- Start to teach sit when your puppy is around eight weeks old.
- Be consistent and firm as you teach.
- Bring a special treat to the first few training sessions, such as chicken or Cheerios.

Once you are prepared, you can get started working and bonding with your cute little Pom.

Sit

Once you settle into your quiet training location with the special treat, begin the training. It is relatively easy to train your dog to obey this command. Wait until your puppy starts to sit down and say sit as he or she sits. If your puppy finishes sitting down, start to give praise for it. Naturally, this will make your puppy incredibly excited and wiggly, so it may take a bit of time before he or she will want to sit again. When the time comes and the puppy starts to sit again, repeat the process.

It is going to take more than a couple of sessions for the puppy to fully connect your words with the actions. In fact, it could take a little over a week for your puppy to get it. Poms are intelligent, but at this age there is still so much to learn that the puppy will have a hard time focusing. Commands are something completely new to your little companion. However, once your puppy understands your intention and masters sit, the other commands will likely be a little bit easier to teach.

Once your puppy has demonstrated a mastery over sit, it is time to start teaching down.

Down

Repeat the same process to teach this command as you did for sit. Wait until the puppy starts to lie down, then say the word. If the Pom finishes the action, offer your chosen reward.

It will probably take a little less time to teach this command after you start training it.

Wait until your puppy has mastered down before moving on to stay.

Stay

This command is going to be more difficult since it isn't something that your puppy does naturally. Be prepared for it to take a bit longer to train on this command. It is also important that your dog has mastered and will consistently sit and lie down on command before you start to teach stay.

Choose which of these two commands you want to use to get started, and then you will need to be consistent. Once your dog understands stay for either sit or down, you can train with the second command. Just make sure the first position is mastered before trying the second.

Tell your puppy to either sit or stay. As you do this, place your hand in front of the puppy's face. Wait until the puppy stops trying to lick your hand before you begin again.

When the puppy settles down, take a step away from the Pomeranian. If your puppy is not moving, say stay and give the puppy the treat and some praise for staying.

Giving the reward to your puppy indicates that the command is over, but you also need to indicate that the command is complete. The puppy has to learn to stay until you say it is okay to leave the spot. Once you give the okay to move, do not give treats. Come should not be used as the okay word as it is a command used for something else.

Repeat these steps, taking more steps further from the puppy after a successful command.

Once your puppy understands stay when you move away, start training to stay even if you are not moving. Extend the amount of time required for the puppy to stay in one spot so that he or she understands that stay ends with the okay command.

When you feel that your puppy has stay mastered, start to train the puppy to come.

Come

This is a command you cannot teach until the puppy has learned the previous commands. The other three commands do not require the puppy to know other commands to get started (it is just easier to train if the puppy already has an understanding of what commands are and how the puppy is expected to react to them).

Before you start, decide if you want to use come or come here for the command. You will need to be consistent in the words you use, so make sure you plan it so that you will intentionally use the right command every time.

Leash the puppy.

Tell the puppy to stay. Move away from the puppy.

Say the command you will use for come and give a gently tug on the leash toward you. As long as you did not use the term to indicate that the stay command was done, your puppy will begin to understand the purpose of your new command. If you used the term to indicate the end of stay, it will confuse your puppy because the Pom will associate the command with being able to move freely.

Repeat these steps, building a larger distance between you and the puppy. Once the puppy seems to get it, remove the leash and start at a close distance. If your puppy does not seem to understand the command, give some visual clues about what you want. For example, you can pat your leg or snap your fingers. As soon as your puppy comes running over to you, offer a reward.

Leave It

This is going to be one of the most difficult commands you will teach your puppy because it goes against both your puppy's instincts and interests. Your puppy wants to keep whatever he or she has, so you are going to have to offer something better. It is essential to teach the command early though, as your Pom is going to be very destructive in the early days. You want to get the trigger in place to convince the puppy to drop things.

You may need to start teaching this command outside of the training area as it has a different starting point.

Start when you have time to dedicate yourself to the lesson. You have to wait until the puppy has something in his or her mouth to drop. Toys are usually best. Offer the puppy a special treat. As the Pom drops the toy, say leave it, and hand over the treat.

This is going to be one of those rare times when you must use a treat because your puppy needs something better to convince him or her to drop the toy. For now, your puppy needs that incentive, something more tempting than what he or she already has before your puppy can learn the command.

This will be one of the two commands that will take the longest to teach (quiet being the other). Be prepared to be patient with your pup. Once your puppy gets it, start to teach leave it with food. This is incredibly important to do because it could save your pooch's life. They are likely to lunge at things that look like food when you are out for a walk, and being so low to the ground, they are probably going to see a lot of food-like things long before you do. This command gets them to drop whatever they are munching on before ingesting it.

Quiet

In the beginning, you can also use treats sparingly to reinforce quiet. If your puppy is barking for no apparent reason tell the puppy to be quiet and place a treat nearby. It is almost guaranteed that the dog will fall silent to sniff the treat, in which case, say good dog or good quiet. It will not take too long for your puppy to understand that quiet means no barking. However, it may take a while for your puppy to learn to fight the urge to bark. Be patient with your puppy because it is difficult to stop doing something that you do naturally. How long did it take you to learn to get up early in the morning or to go to bed at a certain time? It is similar for a Pom to learn not to bark.

Where To Go From Here

These are all the commands that you are likely to need with your Pomeranian, but it isn't a complete list of all of the possible commands that you will need. Every Pom is different, and that means that you may need other commands, particularly since they are smart. Training them to listen to more commands is something they will appreciate because it means time having fun with you and staying mentally engaged.

The commands presented in this chapter are the foundation of training, and the Pom is capable of learning so much more. Just make sure that the tricks that you teach your Pom are not too stressful for the puppy. As your puppy ages, you can start teaching tricks that highlight your puppy's agility. Fetch and other interactive tricks will be ideal because your Pom will want to do them.

CHAPTER 12.
Nutrition

Making sure your puppy or adult Pomeranian gets nutritious meals is as important as making sure you have nutritious meals. Many puppy parents are far more careful about what they feed their little companions than they are about feeding themselves (though this is not recommended – take your own health just as seriously).

The problem is that it is all too easy to give a puppy food that the puppy should not be eating, especially food that comes from your plate. This isn't referring to food on the "do not feed list," but the food that is high in calories that your Pom shouldn't be eating because of how small your puppy is or how unhealthy the food is (including for you). As your pup gets older, this can become a serious issue. Given the Pom's tiny size, you have to be careful even about the kind of commercial dog food you purchase (even if you supplement it with homemade food). Ensuring your cute little Pom gets the right nutritional balance is critical for helping your puppy live a long, happy, healthy life. They can live up to 16 years, so making sure they get the right food is how you can keep your loving companion around as long as possible.

CHAPTER 12   Nutrition

Why A Healthy Diet Is Important

Although they have a considerable amount of energy, Pomeranians are a very small breed. Over feeding them is incredibly easy to do because they do not need a whole lot of food before they reach their caloric needs for the day. Many of the tricks and activities that they do can expend a good bit of energy, but that does not mean that they need a lot of food. If you have a very busy schedule, it will be entirely too easy to have substantial lapses in activity levels while you are home. Your Pomeranian is still going to expect the same amount of food, regardless of activity level. This means they are likely to start putting on weight, which will be detrimental to their health.

HELPFUL TIP
Chilly Treat

Fancy treats for dogs abound at any pet store, but there's one popular dog treat that you can make at home for next to nothing. Ice cubes are beloved by many dogs. Putting ice cubes in water on hot summer days, or giving individual ice cubes as treats are both good options. Be aware that aggressive chewers may be at risk of breaking teeth when chewing ice cubes. If your dog chews aggressively, consider making or purchasing alternative frozen treats with a softer texture or using crushed ice instead of cubes.

You need to not only be careful of how much you feed your Pom during mealtime, but how many treats you offer over the course of the day. All food needs to be considered when you consider both nutritional and caloric intake. With those tiny little bodies, you need to be aware of roughly how many calories your dog eats a day. If you notice that your dog is putting on weight, you will be able to adjust how much food the Pomeranian eats a day, or change the food to something with more nutritional value but with fewer calories.

Breeders also recommend that you avoid food made of grains. Grains can make them gain weight faster. If you have the time, it is best to make your dog's meals – or at the least provide real food mixed with their dog food.

Commercial Food

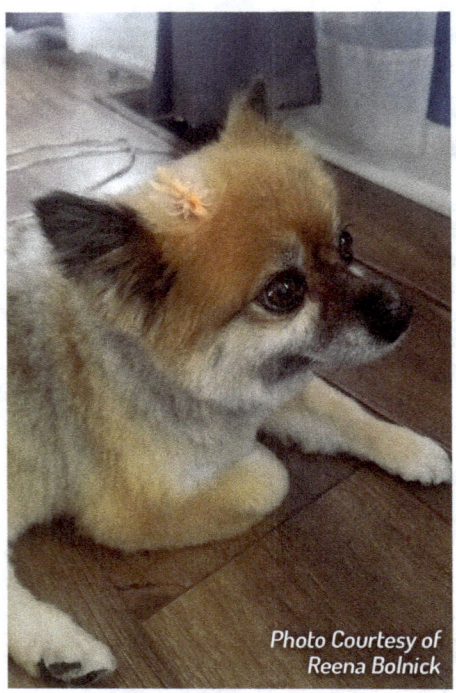
Photo Courtesy of Reena Bolnick

Although it is convenient, commercial dog food is a flawed product. There is nothing natural about those little bits of food you are feeding your dog, and ultimately, it is often not as healthy as making your dog's meals. However, for most people it is the option that will be chosen because preparing every meal is a very lengthy process. For some people, there simply isn't adequate time in the day to make every meal.

If you are one of the majority of puppy parents, make sure that you are buying the best dog food that you can. Take the time to research each of your options, particularly the nutritional value of the food. Always account for your dog's small stature, energy levels, and age. Your puppy may not need puppy food as long as other breeds (or even other Poms), and dog food for seniors may not be the best option for your senior Pomeranian. To provide more nutrition, you can mix some real food into the processed food. This can help supplement any nutrients, as well as being a healthy addition to an otherwise entirely processed meal. The addition of a little bit of home-cooked food with each meal will make your Pomeranian excited to eat.

Pawster provides several great articles about which commercial dog foods are good for Pomeranians. Since new foods come on the market, you will likely want to check back with them to see if there are newer, better foods once a year or every other year. Since you have to be careful of your Pom's weight, it is well worth verifying that you are giving them some of the best foods for their needs.

CHAPTER 12   Nutrition

Preparing Your Food Naturally At Home

If you want to provide the healthiest meals possible, you should plan to spend an extra five to ten minutes in the kitchen per meal you prepare for your Pomeranian. If you regularly make your own food (from scratch, not with a microwave or boxed meal), it really doesn't take that much more time to provide an equally healthy meal for your little companion.

Keeping in mind the foods that your Pomeranian absolutely should not eat, you can mix some of the food you make for yourself in your Pomeranian's meal. Just make sure to add a bit more of what your Pomeranian needs to the puppy food bowl. Although you and your Pom have distinctly different dietary needs, you can tailor your foods to include nutrients that your dog needs. It won't really take that much longer to tailor a meal for you and a slightly different version for your dog. Read through Chapter 4 to make sure that you never give your Pomeranian food that could be harmful or deadly.

Do not feed your Pomeranian from your plate. Split the food, placing your dog's meal into a bowl so that your canine understands that your food is just for you. The best home-cooked meals should be planned in advance so that your Pomeranian is getting the right nutritional balance.

Typically, 50% of your dog's food should be animal protein (fish, poultry, and organ meats). About 25% should be full of complex carbohydrates. The remaining 25% should be from fruits and vegetables, particularly foods like pumpkin, apples, bananas, and green beans. These provide additional flavor that your Pomeranian will probably love while making the little pup feel full faster so that the chance of overeating is reduced.

If you are interested in making meals specifically for your Pom, there are a couple of sites that post new recipes, as well as a couple of pages with several interesting foods to try:

- Pomeranian.org
- Pet Pom
- Pommy Mommy
- Pet Coach
- Dogsaholic (good for many different dog breeds, not just Poms)

Puppy Food Vs. People Food

Photo Courtesy of Amy Casperson

It is true that puppies need more calories than adult dogs, and with their small size, Pomeranian puppies do not need nearly as much as you may think they do to meet caloric needs for their energy levels. If you are bringing a Pomeranian puppy into your home and know that you aren't going to have the time to cook, you should get food designed for puppies. This will ensure that your puppy gets the necessary calories for growth. Do not feed the puppy people food under the belief that you can switch to dog food later – because that is going to be virtually impossible later. Once your Pomeranian becomes an adult, it is nearly impossible to convince your canine that those unappetizing pellets are food, particularly when your dog knows what the food on your plate tastes like. Do not set a precedent that will create significant problems for yourself later. If you feed your Pom home-cooked food, you are going to have to keep making food for your dog once the puppy stage is a memory.

It is best to make your puppy's food if you can. There really isn't going to be that much of a difference in the amount of food between the puppy and adult stages. Their little bodies have special needs, and the first few months are critical. If you can make your puppy's meals (and know that you can keep it up when your Pom is an adult), this will be a lot healthier for your dog.

If you find that you have to start buying commercial food, you will need to start slowly mixing it into your adult dog's meal. Do not be surprised if you find the pellets are uneaten for a while. It will be a difficult process convincing your dog that this is food, but if you mix it with other things (and know that you are always going to need to mix at least a little real food in with the commercial food), your dog will be more likely to start eating it since it will smell like real food.

CHAPTER 12   Nutrition

Weight Management

"Pomeranians do not need much exercise. Just following you around the house or yard as you go about your tasks is enough for a small Pomeranian."

Kim Howard
TK Kennels

You have to be careful of your Pomeranian's weight, so you need to get used to monitoring it, particularly once your dog is an adult. Your Pom is not going to diet the way you may choose to diet. This means you have to keep a regular eating schedule for your dog – their day is going to be based largely on the times of the day that are designated to eating. If treats and snacks are something you establish as normal early on, your dog is going to believe that is also a part of the routine and will expect it. Obviously, this can be a terrible habit to establish with your Pomeranian, especially if it is food that you are sharing because you are snacking and feel guilty. You will need to make sure to be active after snacking so that your Pom doesn't get too many calories. An extra round of play or another walk can go a long way to helping keep your Pomeranian at a healthy weight.

There needs to be a healthy balance of diet and exercise to keep your Pomeranian from becoming overweight, certainly to avoid your dog becoming obese. Exercise is an absolute must. While you are helping your Pomeranian develop healthy eating and exercise habits, you are probably helping yourself. Being more aware of your dog's diet and exercise levels will probably make you more aware of your own. Obesity is something that you will need to actively avoid with a small dog. Get used to exercising and playing as a reward system.

Weighing your Pomeranian will be incredibly helpful to ensuring that the pooch is staying at a healthy weight. Because they are really toy sized, you can use your own scales to weigh them. Gently pick up your canine and step on the scale. Subtract your weight from the total, and that is how much your Pomeranian weighs. Be honest about your weight. That means weighing yourself just before weighing your Pom, and being accurate with the number. Counting calories is quite time consuming, but you should also know roughly how many calories your Pomeranian eats in a day because it really does not take much to meet the needs of such a small dog.

CHAPTER 13.
Exercising – So Easy, Yet So Critical

Photo Courtesy of Elizabeth Marciano

Since Poms do tend to be fairly intelligent, you can also expend that energy through training. The more they learn, the more energetic the next trick can be. Games like fetch or hide and seek can really wear out a Pomeranian, and you don't need a whole lot of space for either of these activities. With several hundred years of being companions to humans coupled with their roots in working with humans, they are incredibly loyal. Any time you want to spend with them playing, training, or just getting out for a walk is okay with them, giving you a lot of options for engaging with your canine in ways that work for any size home or any weather condition. If you want to go somewhere, your Pomeranian will very likely enjoy a new environment and experience.

Playing inside to get the rest of your Pom's exercise will be a breeze. It will become an easy way of relieving stress and bonding with your little family member. This helps your pup to burn off some of the calories while showing that you are happy to reciprocate play time. You do need to make sure that they get enough exercise daily because you don't want them to be a bundle of energy at the day's end. Because their legs are so much shorter, they will expend a lot more energy on those walks than you will, which makes a 30-minute evening walk very efficient in getting them to be tired enough to want to go to bed.

Obviously, they don't make a great jogging companion because there is pretty much no hope that they will be able to keep up with a human who is jogging. Stick with walks and indoor play to help tire your darling.

CHAPTER 13   Exercising – So Easy, Yet So Critical

Photo Courtesy of
Casey Taylor-Racinelli

Exercise – Essential Need To Stay Active

"Pups will play hard for a short while then nap. This is normal. They are babies. They need to rest & sleep just like human babies. They need exercise, affection & playtime when they are awake."

Gary & Janie Burnette
Burnette's Exclusive Pomeranians

Photo Courtesy of S Renee Pulse

Exercise will be fairly simple during the first month. Taking short, frequent walks while your Pom gets accustomed to the harness and leash will help you prepare for longer walks as much as it prepares the puppy. Playing will be a lot easier because you don't have to harness the Pom up. You can strike a good balance between walks and play in the early days to help keep your puppy expending his energy.

Other people and dogs can be great helpers when it comes to puppy training – especially adult dogs. Things are much easier for the puppy to understand when an adult dog does it first.

Make sure that the leash is a good fit. Your Pom probably isn't going to be able to break it (unless it is an old, frayed leash), but they can be incredibly fast when it comes to working off collars and leashes and taking off harnesses. You can bring this up with the vet to make sure the harness is properly securing your Pom.

CHAPTER 13   Exercising – So Easy, Yet So Critical

Photo Courtesy of Tanya Willard

Photo Courtesy of Rachel Lubbe

Playtime!

Playing with Poms is easy to do, and it can be almost addictive because of the amount of enthusiasm they have, and how adorable they are during playtime. Your Pomeranian is probably going to be ready to play whenever you make any indication that it is play time. Have a toy or words ready, and your Pomeranian will be more than ready to do whatever you want to do. Of course, your Pomeranian will likely try to initiate playtime too.

Put aside some time to look over all of the recommendations online for games to play with Pomeranians, as well as great tricks for them. As your puppy grows and learns, you'll be able to add new tricks and games so that you can keep them mentally stimulated. It may not take much to tire them because of their size, but a bored dog can be problematic too. Keeping your Pom from getting bored can help keep them from getting into trouble, as well as being a great way to bond with them.

CHAPTER 13 Exercising – So Easy, Yet So Critical

One of the best games for a Pomeranian is hide and seek. They have tons of energy and will love looking for you. It will give them short bursts of activity, and you will be able to gauge when they are finally too tired and stop. You will need to teach your pup Stay to get the best results, but in the early day, if you can set a distraction and leave while your pup is busy, and you will have time to hide. Remember they are short and stay where they can find you (don't hide too high off the ground).

Like hide and seek, bubbles are a great distraction/game for Pomeranians. Simply blow the bubbles, and your little puppy will learn to chase down those bubbles. It takes very little of your energy, but can quickly tire a young puppy if each round has several bubbles.

Set up your own obstacle course inside. They are a tiny breed, so it really doesn't take that much to have them complete a course, even when they are young. Obviously a puppy isn't going to be able to do complicated courses, but even running over a couple of pillows and jumping through your arms can make them very tired. You can also use toys and blankets to change up the course.

Tug of war is a classic game, and one that your little puppy will play without having to learn, or can learn quickly if your puppy is one of the rare pups that isn't inclined to latch on and play. Despite their size, they almost always think they will win. And they tend to be right since it is difficult to see that little face be disappointed. You can use a small toy, towel, or even old shirt for this game. It will need to be soft and small to fit in that adorable mouth. It is funny to watch them never want to give up, and you probably play until your puppy finally wins if you don't let the little guy win in those early days.

CHAPTER 14.
Grooming – Productive Bonding

"Pomeranians, especially a high quality one will shed lots. Brush, brush, brush."

Fatihah Mach
Lunar Poms

Pomeranians have two layers to their coat, which means you are going to need to dedicate time to managing it every day. Fortunately, this is not only an easy chore to do, but given how happy your Pom will be to spend that kind of time with you, this is going to be a chore that you don't mind doing.

Grooming always goes beyond just coat maintenance though, and that is true for all dogs. You also need to regularly care for their nails, teeth, eyes, and ears. Fortunately, this is fairly easy for Poms as they aren't prone to problems with them. As long as you regularly brush your pup's teeth and monitor their eyes and ears to ensure they are healthy, Poms are incredibly easy to groom.

Your Pom's grooming needs include the following:
- Coat (bath and brushing)
- Nails
- Eyes and ears
- Teeth

If you do not have time to properly groom your Pomeranian, then establish a regular appointment with a groomer. Baths and trimmings may be best left to a professional. Things like daily brushings (coat and teeth) are things you are going to need to make time to do. Fortunately, they are not time consuming since Poms are so small.

CHAPTER 14   Grooming – Productive Bonding

Grooming Tools

"Pomeranians do shed, sometimes a lot. Shedding is worse when shedding their winter coats during hot weather. Females shed tremendously after a heat cycle or a litter of puppies. If Pomeranians are kept mostly inside and are neutered/spayed the shedding is minimal."

Kim Howard
TK Kennels

If you plan to groom your Pom yourself, make sure you know how best to do all of the exercises before you first attempt them. You will need the following tools to properly groom your Pom:
- Shampoo (check Pawster for the latest recommendations)
- Pin or slicker brush
- Small nail trimmers
- Toothbrush and toothpaste (check Pawster for the latest recommendations)

Managing Your Pomeranian's Coat

The Pomeranian coat is part of the attraction for many people because it is a truly beautiful coat. Some people say that Poms don't shed, which is completely false – all dogs with double coats shed. Because they are small, Poms don't shed that much. As long as you make brushing a regular part of your day, you aren't going to have an issue with shedding.

Puppy

"It is not recommended to cut their fur down to the 'Boo' look because the long whips of fur captures cool air & keeps their body regulated. Poms can sunburn if shaved down too close to skin."

Gary & Janie Burnette
Burnette's Exclusive Pomeranians

Brushing a puppy is going to take you more time than brushing an adult because of the excitement and attention the puppy feels. There will be a lot of wiggling and attempts at play. Trying to tell your puppy that the brush is not a toy clearly isn't going to work, so be prepared to be patient during each brushing session. On the other hand, they are so adorable, you prob-

CHAPTER 14   Grooming – Productive Bonding

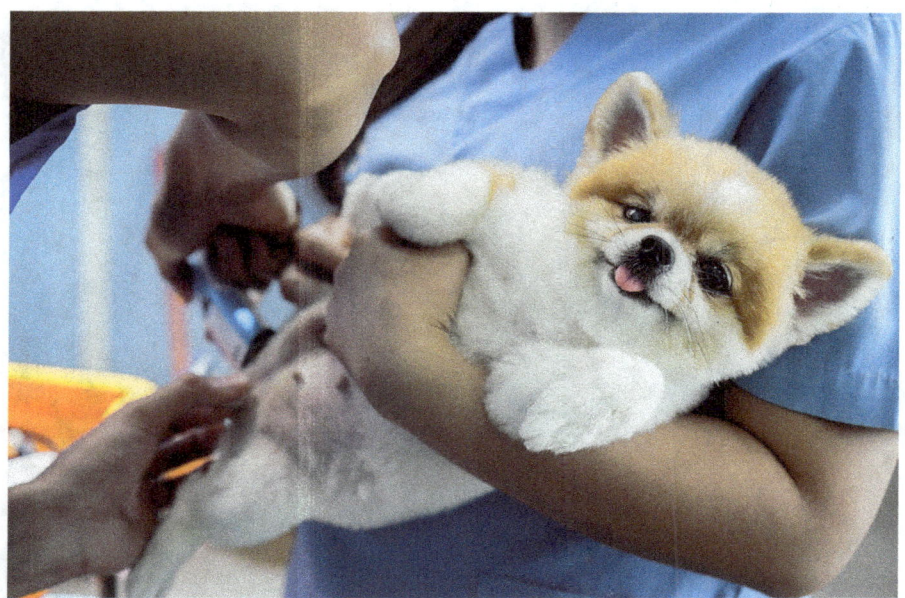

ably won't mind that it takes a bit longer. Just make sure you let your pup know that this is a serious effort and playing comes after it. Otherwise, your Pom is going to always try to play, which will make brushing your dog a lot more time consuming. You definitely want to curb any idea that will give your Pom a reason to be stubborn about behaving.

You can plan to brush your puppy after a vigorous exercise so that your Pom has far less energy to fight or play. Be careful that you don't encourage rambunctious behavior during brushing because this will become part of the routine, and your Pomeranian will think that the brush is meant for playtime, and it is going to be difficult to convince him that it isn't true the longer it happens. Maybe you won't mind in the beginning, but there will be times when you just want to finish brushing your dog

HELPFUL TIP
Coat-Conditioner Spray

Pomeranians are long-haired dogs and can therefore be prone to tangles in their fur. To maintain a healthy coat, you'll need to brush your Pomeranian regularly. If your dog's fur is knotted, it will be easier and more comfortable for you and your dog to use a coat conditioning or detangling spray before brushing. There are a number of commercial options available for this kind of spray, or it can be created at home using a dog conditioner and water in a spray bottle. Spritz this solution onto your dog's fur before brushing with the appropriate brush.

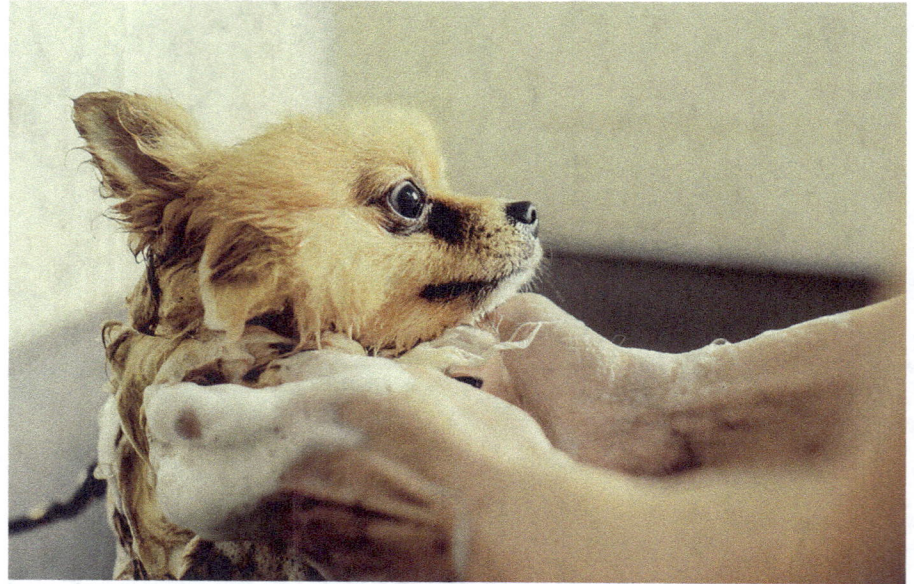

quickly, and that is why you need to make sure your puppy doesn't think it is time to play.

As you get accustomed to brushing your puppy, get accustomed to checking his skin. Look for rashes, sores, or infections. You should also check his eyes, ears, and mouth while you are grooming him. Keep doing these activities even after your Pom is an adult. Since this breed has such small bodies, it won't be that time consuming, and it will help you to spot potential issues as early as possible.

Adulthood

Adults can be brushed every day, but they should be brushed at least a few times a week. With long fur that is really thick, that coat can get matted and dirty quickly. Daily brushing will help you better manage the fur so that it doesn't tangle or become matted. If you properly train your puppy how to behave, this will be incredibly easy.

If you rescued an adult, it may take a little while to get the dog used to being brushed frequently. If you aren't able to get your dog to feel comfortable with the brushings in the beginning, you can work it into your schedule, like training. As your Pom gets more comfortable with the surroundings, it will be easier to brush them daily.

CHAPTER 14   Grooming – Productive Bonding

You can also have their coats cut or trimmed regularly if you would like. It is best to learn h0w to do this from a groomer before you try to do it yourself.

Cleaning Their Eyes And Ears

When you bathe your Pomeranian, you need to be careful not to get water in their ears. You should also make a habit of regularly checking their eyes and ears.

As they age, Pomeranians may develop cataracts, but that is a fairly common problem for all dogs. You can generally tell if a dog is older because it will have a cloudy look in their eyes. You can have your Pom checked to make sure your little dear isn't developing cataracts. If your canine is, you many need to take the pup in to have them removed as cataracts can lead to blindness.

Their ears should never appear to be red inside. Getting the interior of the ears wet can lead to infection and other problems. Be careful when you bathe your pup, and finish with a quick ear check to make sure that they are still healthy.

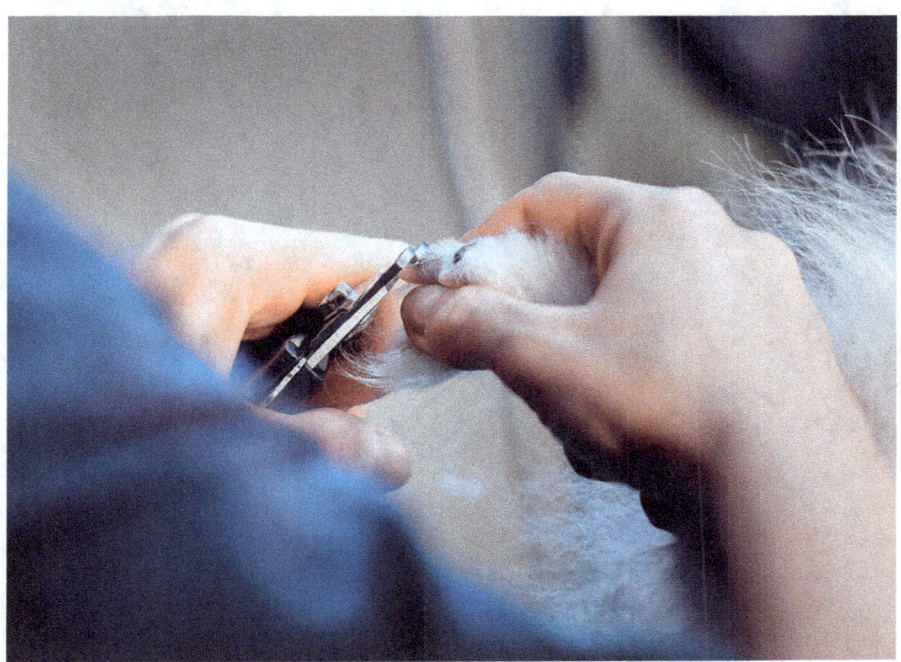

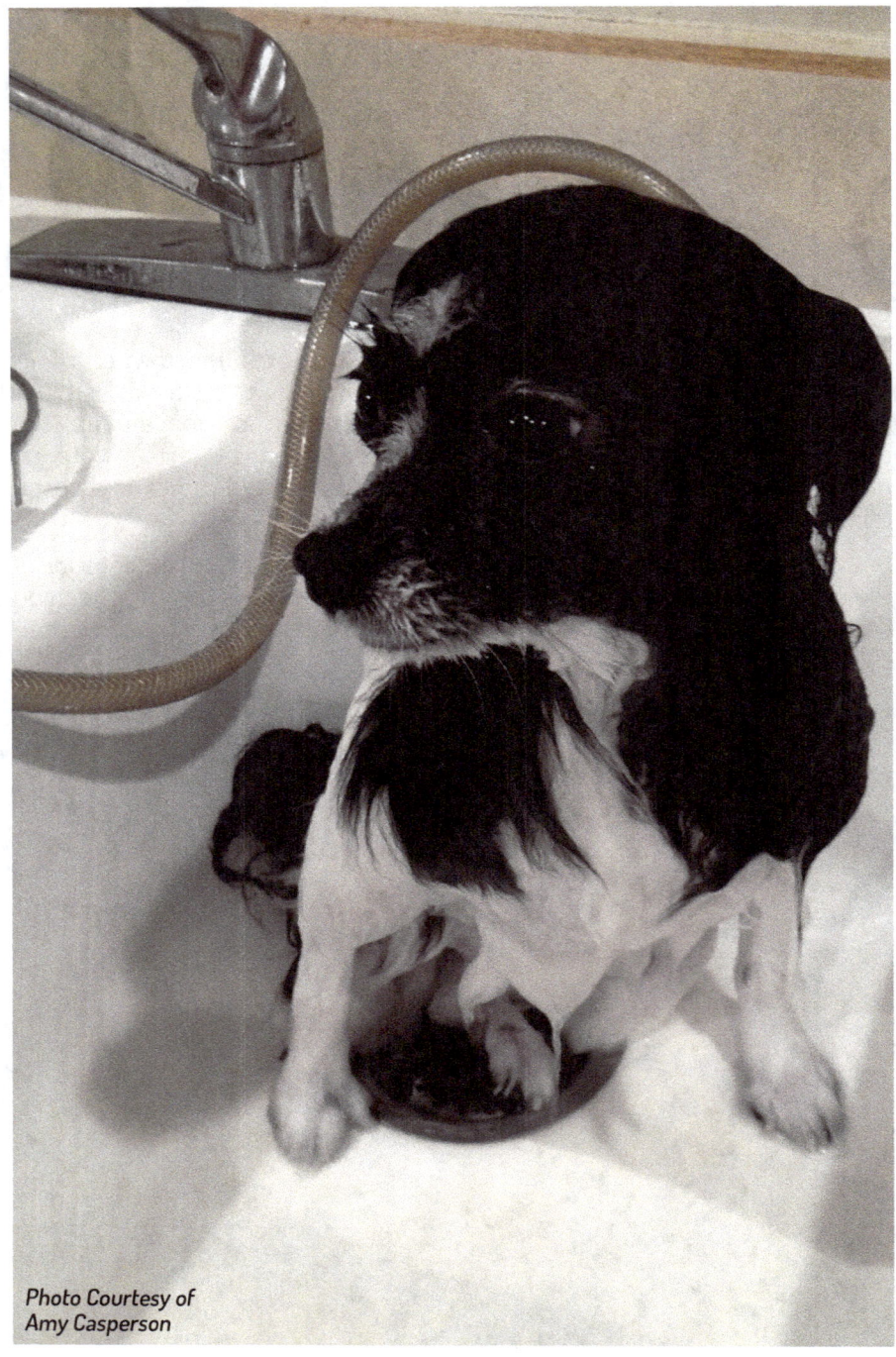

Photo Courtesy of Amy Casperson

CHAPTER 14   Grooming – Productive Bonding

Bath Time

Bath time shouldn't be a problem, at least not from a frequency perspective. Every few months should be more than enough to keep your pup clean, especially if you are brushing him daily. Set your bath schedule for about once a quarter (four times a year), and your puppy should be happy. Of course, if your Pom gets dirty, then you will need to take the time to bathe your canine.

Trimming The Nails

Pomeranian toenails should not be long enough to click when they walk on hard floors or concrete. Take them in to have those little nails cut at least twice a month. Pay attention to the sounds your dog makes when walking on harder surfaces to make sure that the nails aren't clicking. If they are, then you should increase how often you get the nails cut.

Poms have tiny paws and a lot of fur. Both of these can make it difficult to cut their nails if you don't have much experience. When you add how stubborn they can be, it is best to leave cutting the nails up to a professional.

Brushing Their Teeth

Check with your vet to see what a good toothpaste to use would be to brush your pup's teeth. Make sure to brush their teeth at least once a week to ensure they don't develop trouble with their gums when they get older. This is good practice for all dogs, so if you already have other canines, have them all on the same weekly brushing schedule.

If you aren't sure what to do, there are several tutorials online that you can use to get an idea of how to get around your Pom's struggle to get away during the process. Like brushing the coat, Poms need their teeth brushed often to avoid dental problems, and you probably will want to learn to do it yourself over having to visit a shop once a week. It is also nice to know how to do it if their breath smells bad or if they manage to eat something that smells foul.

CHAPTER 15.
Health Care

The reason Poms have remained so popular over the centuries is because of how loving, loyal, and adorable they are. As long as you are careful and take good care of your little buddy, you will have well over a decade to enjoy your exuberant little companion. With such curiosity and enthusiasm to learn, your Pomeranian may not let you know if something hurts. This is particularly bad since they are not a sturdy dog. While it is one reason to make sure no one plays too rough with your canine, it also means that they may not let you know if they have another type of problem – fleas or ticks.

In addition to making sure your canine doesn't get hurt through rambunctious play, there are some basic preventative measures you should take to make sure your puppy stays healthy. Many of the treatments and concerns are universal across the entire canine world, which means there is a good chance you already know that you need to take care of your small dog. You can consider this chapter as more of a reminder or checklist of things you probably already know you need to be aware of. Treating and keeping your puppy free of parasites should be something that you add to your budget once they are old enough for the treatments.

Photo Courtesy of Stacey Papo

CHAPTER 15   Health Care

Fleas And Ticks

Since Poms don't require much outdoor time, they are at a lower risk of getting ticks. Fleas are something that you will need to watch for since they live in yards too. Your little Pom is going to be outside some of the time, which means you still have to monitor him. If your Pom loves roaming through high grass, you cannot allow any lapse in treatment, even in winter.

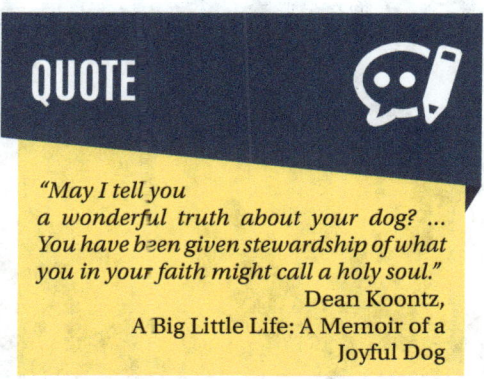

QUOTE

"May I tell you a wonderful truth about your dog? ... You have been given stewardship of what you in your faith might call a holy soul."
Dean Koontz,
A Big Little Life: A Memoir of a Joyful Dog

With each bath you give your Pom, make time to check for ticks and fleas as part of the cleaning process. Comb through the fur and check the skin for irritation and parasites. This will help keep your puppy healthier and feeling much better. Since you will be doing this often, you should be able to know when a bump is a problem. Since your dog will be very happy to spend time with you, it shouldn't take as long as you think – it isn't as though you will have to spend a lot of time struggling to get your Pom to sit still for a tick check.

Fleas will be more problematic because they are far more mobile. The best way to look for fleas is to make it a regular part of your brushing sessions. You can also look for behavioral indicators, such as incessant scratching and licking. With the regular checks on your pup's skin when brushing his or her hair, you will be able to check the spots where your dog is scratching to see if the skin is irritated or if it is the work of a flea. Given the small stature of your companion, fleas will have no trouble jumping on your Pom from the grass or other vegetation. This means you will need to use flea preventative products on a regular basis. You won't be able to do this with puppies under a certain age, but once they mature, you can start adding treatment to the budget and schedule.

If you want to use natural products instead of the chemical filled products, set aside a few hours to research the alternatives and find out what works best for your Pom. Do not increase the number of baths because their skin is sensitive and should not be washed too often, so increasing the frequency of baths should not be part of the solution. Do verify that any natural product purchases work before you buy them.

Remedies should be applied monthly. Establishing a regular schedule and adding it to the calendar will help you remember to treat your dog on schedule.

Worms And Parasites

Photo Courtesy of Debbie Deardorf

Although worms and other types of parasites are a less common problem than fleas and ticks, they can be far more dangerous. There are a number of types of worms that you should be aware of:

- Heartworms
- Hookworms
- Roundworms
- Tapeworms
- Whipworms

One of the primary problems is that there isn't an easy to recognize set of symptoms to help identify when your dog has a problem with worms. However, you can keep an eye out for these symptoms, and if your dog shows them, you should schedule a visit to the vet.

- If your Pomeranian is unexpectedly lethargic for at least a few days.
- Patches of fur begin to fall out (this will be noticeable if you brush your Pomeranian regularly) or if you notice patchy spaces in your dog's coat.
- If your dog's stomach becomes distended (expands), set up an appointment immediately to have him or her checked. Your dog's stomach will look like a potbelly.
- Your Pomeranian begins coughing, vomiting, has diarrhea, or has a loss in appetite.

These symptoms should be more obvious in a Pom because they tend to be active or with you all of the time. If you aren't sure, it is best to get to the vet as soon as possible to check.

If your dog has hookworms or roundworms, you will also need to visit a doctor to get checked. These worms can be spread to you from your dog through skin contact. If your dog has them, you are at risk of contracting them. Being treated at the same time can help stop the vicious cycle of continually switching which of you has worms.

CHAPTER 15   Health Care

Heartworms are a significant threat to your dog's health as they can be deadly. You should be actively treating your dog to ensure that this parasite does not have a home in your dog. There are medications that can ensure your Pom does not get or have heartworms.

Benefits Of Veterinarians

Your dog should have regular visits to your vet, just like you have regular checkups for yourself. From regular shots to health checkups, vets will make sure that your Pom stays healthy. With a number of potential issues, you want to make sure that your Pom doesn't have any of the many possible problems.

Since Poms are such eager companions, it is going to be obvious when they aren't acting normal. Annual visits to the vet will ensure there isn't a problem that is slowly draining the energy or health from your dog.

Health checkups also make sure that your Pom is aging well. If there are any early symptoms of something potentially wrong with your dog over the years (such as arthritis), you will be able to start making adjustments. The vet can help you come up with ways to manage pain and problems that come with the aging process. Your vet will be able to recommend adjustments to the schedule to accommodate your canine's aging body and diminishing abilities. This will ensure that you can keep having fun together without hurting your dog. These changes are well worth it in the end because your dog will be able to keep enjoying time with you without suffering additional pain.

Photo Courtesy of Christina Getscher

Holistic Alternatives

Wanting to keep a dog from a lot of exposure to chemical treatments makes sense, and there are many good reasons why people are moving to more holistic methods. However, doing this does require a lot more research and monitoring to ensure that the methods are working – and more importantly, do not harm your dog. Unverified holistic medicines can be a waste of money, or, worse, they can even be harmful to your pet. Other methods have often been used for far longer, so there is more data to ensure that they aren't doing more harm than good. However, natural methods that work are always preferable to any chemical solution.

If you decide to go with holistic medication, talk with your vet about your options. You can also seek out Pom experts to see what they recommend

Photo Courtesy of Kat O'Brien

CHAPTER 15　Health Care

before you start using any methods you are interested in trying. Read what scientists have said about the medicine. There is a chance that the products you buy from a store are actually better than some holistic medications.

Make sure you are thorough in your research and that you do not take any unnecessary risks with the health of your Pom.

Vaccinating Your Pomeranian

Vaccination schedules are almost universal for all dog breeds, including Pomeranians. The following list can help you ensure your Pom receives necessary shots on schedule. Make sure to add this to your calendar
- The first shots are required at between 6 and 8 weeks following the birth of your Pom. You should find out from the breeder if these shots have been taken care of and get the records of the shots:
  - Corona virus
  - Distemper
  - Hepatitis
  - Leptospirosis
  - Parainfluenza
  - Parvo
- These same shots are required again at between 10 and 12 weeks of age.
- These same shots are required again at between 14 and 15 weeks old, as well as his or her first rabies shot.
- Your dog will need to get these shots annually after that. Your Pomeranian will also need annual rabies shots afterward.

Once you start the shots, you need to see them through to the end. Make sure to get the schedule for upkeep on these shots. Then you will need to maintain these shots over the years, particularly shots like rabies.

CHAPTER 16.
Health Concerns

STORY
Another Chance

Real Housewives of Beverly Hills star Lisa Vanderpump is an advocate for Pomeranians with alopecia. Her family founded the 501c3 Vanderpump Dog Foundation in 2016 to improve the lives of dogs both domestically and internationally. Mrs. Vanderpump owns several Pomeranians, at least one of whom was rescued. In 2016, the Sacramento SPCA tagged Vanderpump in a Twitter post about a Pomeranian who had been surrendered to them just after Christmas in 2015 and who suffered from alopecia. Vanderpump adopted the dog and named him Prince Harry.

The problem with all purebred dogs, including Pomeranians, is that they are prone to predictable ailments because of inbreeding. Breeders now actively work to ensure these kinds of problems are not perpetuated as much as possible, but you still have to be aware of the potential problems because there is no guarantee that your canine won't have some of the genetic issues. Good breeders offer guarantees to ensure their puppies will be returned if they have one of the known genetic issues with the breed. To meet the requirements of these guarantees that means you have to know the problems and their symptoms.

The sooner you start to counter any potential problems, the longer your Pom is likely to live and the healthier he or she is likely to be. This means more time enjoying each other's company. If you notice any of the symptoms listed in the earlier chapters, make sure to schedule an appointment with your vet to have your dog checked.

Adopting a puppy can give you the span of a dog's entire life to ensure your dog is as healthy as possible. The breeder should be able to provide health records in addition to any shot records and required tests. All of the details on the genetic and common ailments of Pomeranian are in Chapter 3. Making sure that the parents are healthy increases the likelihood that your puppy will remain healthy over his or her entire life. However, there is still a chance that your dog will have one of these documented problems even if the parents don't, so you will still need to keep an eye on your little friend.

CHAPTER 16   Health Concerns

A Dog With A Lot Of Possible Health Concerns

Some breeders will say that Poms are a healthy breed. Others say that they aren't. This kind of inconsistency shows just how much of a variable genetics are.

There are two primary concerns that require your attention – your dog's face and that adorable, fragile body.

Face

The Pom's face is very distinctive, looking more like a fox than nearly any other dog breed. You have to make sure to keep the hair around their face trimmed to keep dirt from getting into their eyes. They can also develop gum disease if you don't regularly brush their teeth. With such little mouths, their teeth can overcrowd too, so if you have a puppy, you need to make sure to regularly brush their teeth (a bit more often than as an adult) to keep them from collecting food and other particles between their teeth.

Body

The Pomeranian's body looks study, but under all of that fur, your dog is actually pretty fragile. They can't handle you playing rough with them. Playing with Poms is encouraged, but you always need to make sure that playtime does not include roughhousing. They can have problems with their hind quarters, so you need to be very mindful of arthritis and other problems as your Pom ages.

Photo Courtesy of Debbie Deardorf

Pomeranians may also be affected by Severe Hair Loss Syndrome as they get older. It more often happens in males as they reach their golden years. Over time, their coat gets thinner. Watch the back of their thighs to see if this is happening. Talk with your vet if you notice that their back legs start to lose hair at a faster rate than when they were young.

Photo Courtesy of Kassie Lamontagne

CHAPTER 16 Health Concerns

Typical Purebred Health Issues

"Some Poms have been developing Black Skin Disease, commonly called BSD. They lose most of their coat and it doesn't grow back. Other than that, it doesn't hurt the dog and is not painful."

Claudia Wallen
Pearl Moon Poms

Small dogs tend to be notorious for their health problems, and unfortunately this is true of Pomeranians. They tend to be a healthy breed, with the oldest living over 16 years, but the genetic health problems that they can have are serious.

- Legg-Calve-Perthes disease is a hip condition that causes your pup's blood supply to the rear legs to be reduced. If you notice your Pom start limping at between 4 and 6 months, consult your vet about the possibility of this problem.
- Progressive retinal atrophy and tear duct issues that you need to watch for in your canine.
- There are several heart conditions that may affect young Poms. Make sure to discuss these with the breeder before bringing your puppy home.
- Luxating patellas happens when your canine's kneecaps slip out of place. During your regular visits, have your vet check their knees. If you notice your Pom limping, set up an appointment to have the little guy checked out to make sure this isn't the problem.

In addition to these problems, you have to be aware of the problems that arise from their small stature.

- Their necks are fragile, which means you have to be careful when you walk them, even when you put a collar on them. If their collar is too tight, or if you pull them too hard on a walk, their trachea can collapse. This will make it difficult for your dog to breathe.
- Their small mouths make it easy for their teeth to overcrowd, which can trap food. Regular brushing should always be taken seriously to ensure that they don't have any food remaining in their teeth. It is also good to remove plaque.

Photo Courtesy of Penny Hall

Where You Can Go Wrong

In addition to genetic problems, there are things that you can do that could damage your dog's health. These are related to the dog's diet and exercise levels. If you follow the recommendations in Chapter 15, your dog will remain healthy longer.

Importance Of Breeder To Ensuring Health In Your Pomeranian

Being aware of the health of the parents and the diseases that are known to be a problem for them or their parents will help you know what to monitor for in your Pom.

Any breeder that doesn't provide a health guarantee for a breed as established as the Pom is not a breeder you should consider getting a dog from. Avoid all of these breeders – they are interested in the money, and the dog's health is of little to no concern. If a breeder says that a puppy or litter has to be kept in an isolated location for health reasons, do not work with that breeder.

Ask the breeder to talk about the history of the parents, the kinds of health problems that have been in the dog's family, and if the breeder has had problems with any particular illness in the past. If the breeder gives you only short or vague answers, this is a sign that the breeder has dogs that are more likely to have issues later.

CHAPTER 16   Health Concerns

Common Diseases And Conditions

Their size makes them susceptible to some different problems than most breeds. The following are the areas where you need to monitor your Pom:
- Skin
- Breathing
- Eyes
- Teeth
- Coat
- Knees and back legs

Prevention & Monitoring

Beyond genetic issues (something you should learn about the parents before getting your puppy), the problem you have to worry about is weight. Previous chapters provide information about the right diet and exercise for your Pom. Refraining from giving your Pom foods made of grains and keeping their daily caloric intake within a healthy range area are essential because of the dog's size. Considering the fact that they will eat whatever you give them, your dog's weight is always going to be a concern if you aren't careful. Your vet will likely talk to you if your dog has too much weight on its body because this not only puts a strain on the dog's legs, joints, and muscles, it can also have adverse effects on your dog's heart, blood flow, and respiratory system.

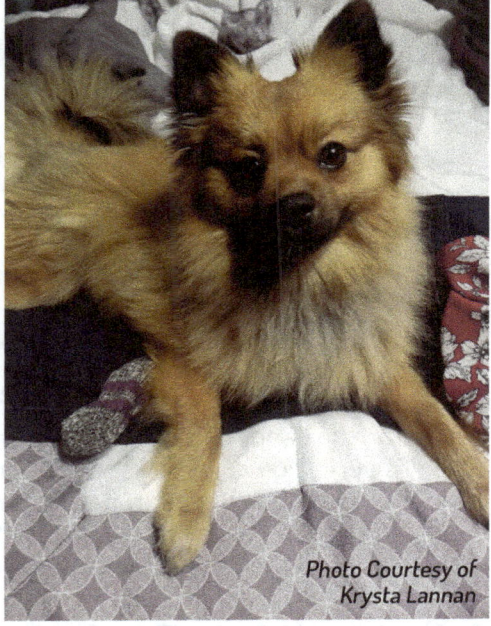

Photo Courtesy of Krysta Lannan

CHAPTER 17.
Your Aging Pomeranian

Photo Courtesy of Debra DeRooy

Pomeranians have a life expectancy of between 12 and 16 years. They are prone to some late in life problems, like hip dysplasia that will mean making some real changes in your life as your dog reaches the golden years. The senior Pom is 9 years old and up. As your dog ages, you will need to start making adjustments to accommodate his or her reduced abilities. A dog may remain healthy his or her entire life, but the body just won't be able to do the same activities at 12 years that it could do at 2. The changes you need to make will be based on your Pom's specific needs. The decline tends to be gradual, just little things here and there, like your Pom having less traction on smooth surfaces. Over time, the body will start to deteriorate so that your dog will not be able to jump as high.

As your Pom's energy and abilities decrease, you need to make sure that he or she is not overdoing it. You should always make sure your dog doesn't over-exercise, but this is even more important for an older dog. Poms may be too focused on having fun to realize they are hurting until they start to rest. These later years will be just as much fun; you will just need to make sure your Pom isn't pushing the new limitations. It is easy to make the senior years incredibly enjoyable for your Pom and yourself by making the necessary adjustments that allow your dog to keep being active without overexertion.

CHAPTER 17   Your Aging Pomeranian

Senior Dog Care

It is usually easier to take care of a senior dog than a young dog, and the Pom is no exception. Naps are just as exciting as walks. Sleeping beside you while you watch television or even if you nap with your dog is pretty much all it takes to make your Pom happy (though that was probably true when they were young too).

However, you must continue to be vigilant about diet and exercise. Now is not the time to let your Pom start to eat anything and everything or neglect to take your regular walks. A senior Pom cannot handle extra weight, so you must be careful to ensure he or she remains healthy with age.

> **QUOTE**
>
> *"Dogs die. But dogs live, too. Right up until they die, they live. They live brave, beautiful lives. They protect their families. And love us. And make our lives a little brighter. And they don't waste time being afraid of tomorrow."*
>
> Dan Gemeinhart,
> The Honest Truth

If your canine cannot manage long walks, make the walks shorter and more numerous and spend more time romping around your yard or home.

When it comes to items that your Pom will need to access regularly, you should make some changes to your current configuration.

- Set water bowls out in a couple of different places so that your dog can easily reach them as needed. If your Pomeranian shows signs of having trouble drinking or eating, you can place slightly raised water dishes around the home to make it easier for him or her to drink.
- Cover hard floor surfaces (such as tiles, hardwood, and vinyl). Use carpets or rugs that will not slip out from under your Pom.
- Add cushions and softer bedding for your Pom. This will both make the surface more comfortable and help your Pom stay warmer. There are some bed warmers for dogs if your Pom displays achy joints or muscles often. Of course, you also need to make sure your Pom isn't too warm, so this can be a fine balancing act.
- Increase how often you brush your Pom to improve his or her circulation. This should be very agreeable to your Pom as a way to make up for other limitations that mean you must do other activities less often.

Photo Courtesy of Amy Casperson

- Stay inside in extreme heat and cold. Your Pom is hardy, but the old canine body cannot handle the extreme changes as well as once it did.
- Use stairs or ramps for your Pom instead of constantly picking up your canine. Picking your Pom up may be more convenient for you, but it is not healthy for you or your Pom. Let your dog maintain a bit more self-sufficiency.
- Avoid changing your furniture around, particularly if your Pom shows signs of having trouble with his or her sight. A familiar home is more comforting and less stressful as your pet ages. If your Pom is not able to see as clearly as he or she once did, keeping the home familiar will make it easier for your dog to move around without getting hurt.
- If you have stairs, consider setting up an area where your dog can stay without having to use the stairs as often.
- Create a space where your Pom can relax with fewer distractions and noises. Your Pom will probably be even less comfortable being left alone for extended periods, but you should have a place where you and your older dog can just relax without loud or startling noises. Don't make your little friend feel isolated, but do give him or her a place to get away from everyone if he needs to be alone.
- Be prepared to let your dog out more often for restroom breaks.

CHAPTER 17 Your Aging Pomeranian

Nutrition

Since a decrease in exercise is inevitable for any aging dog, you will need to adjust your pet's diet. If you opt to feed your Pom commercial dog food, make sure you change to the senior food. If you make your Pom's food, take the time to research how best to reduce calories without sacrificing taste. Your canine is going to need less fat in his or her food, so you may need to find something healthier that still has a lot taste to supplement the types of foods you gave your Pom as a puppy or active adult dog.

Exercise

Exercise will be entirely up to you because your Pom is still just happy to be with you. If you make fewer demands, decrease the number of walks, or in any way change the routine, your Pom will quickly adapt to the new program. It is up to you to adjust the schedule and keep your Pomeranian happily active. Usually increasing the number of walks with shorter durations will help keep your Pom as active as necessary.

Keep in mind that your Pom is more likely to gain weight in the later years, something that his or her body really cannot handle. While the exercise will be reduced, it should not be eliminated. Keep to what your dog can manage and adjust food accordingly to keep the weight healthy.

Photo Courtesy of Linda Damiano

This will probably be the hardest part of watching your Pomeranian age. However, you will need to watch your Pom for signs of tiredness or pain so that you can stop exercising before your dog has done too much. Your pace will need to be slower and your attention more on your dog, but ultimately it can be just as exciting. You will probably notice that your Pom spends more time sniffing. This could be a sign that your dog is tiring, or it could be his or her way of acknowledging that long steady walks are a thing of the past and is stopping to enjoy the little things more. It is an interesting time and gives you a chance to get to understand your Pom as the years start to show. Your Pom may also let you know that it is time to go home by turning around to go back or sitting down a lot and looking at you. Take the hint and go home if your Pom lets you know that the limits have been reached.

Mental Stimulation

Unlike the body, your Pomeranian's mind is usually going to be just as sharp and clever in the golden years. That means you can start making adjustments to focus more on the activities that are mentally stimulating. Once your Pom understands the basics, you can start doing training for fun because your Pom will be just as able to learn now as when he or she was 1 year old. Actually, it is likely to be easier because your Pom has learned to focus better and the bond will make him happy to have something he can still do with you.

Your Pom will be grateful for the shift in focus and additional attention. Getting your senior Pomeranian new toys is one way to help keep your dog's mind active if you do not want to train your dog or if you just don't have the time. You can then teach the Pom different names for the toys because it will be fascinating (after all, he or she will still work for praise). Whatever toys you get, make sure they are not too rough on your dog's older jaw and teeth. Tug of war may be a game of the past (you don't want to hurt the old teeth), but other games are still very much appreciated.

Hide and seek is another game that your aging Pom can manage with relative ease. Whether you hide toys or yourself, this can be a game that keeps your Pom guessing.

Regular Vet Exams

Just as humans go to visit the doctor more often as they age, you are going to need to take your dog to see your vet with greater frequency. The vet can make sure that your Pom is staying active without being too active, and that there is no unnecessary stress on your older dog. If your canine has sustained an injury and hidden it from you, your vet is more likely to detect it.

Your vet can also make recommendations about activities and changes to your schedule based on your Pomeranian's physical abilities and any changes in personality. For example, if your Pom is panting more now, it could be a sign of pain from stiffness. This could be difficult to distinguish given how much Poms pant as a rule, but if you see other signs of pain, schedule a visit with the vet. Your vet can help you determine the best way to keep your Pom happy and active during the later years.

Common Old-Age Aliments

Chapters 4 and 16 cover the illnesses that are common or likely with a Pomeranian, but old age tends to bring a slew of ailments that are not particular to any one breed. Here are the things you will need to watch for (as well as talking to your vet about them).

- Diabetes is probably the greatest concern for a breed that loves to eat as much as your Pom does, especially because he has such a small frame. Although it is usually thought of as a genetic condition, any Pom can become diabetic if not fed and exercised properly. It is another reason why it is so important to be careful with your Pom's diet and exercise levels.

- Arthritis is probably the most common ailment in any dog breed, and the Pom is no exception. If your dog is showing signs of stiffness and pain after normal activities, it is very likely that he or she has arthritis. Talk with your vet about safe ways to help minimize the pain and discomfort of this common joint ailment.

- Gum disease is a common issue in older dogs as well, and you should be just as vigilant about brushing teeth when your dog gets older as you do at any other age. A regular check on your Pom's teeth and gums can help ensure this is not a problem.

- Loss of eyesight or blindness is relatively common in older dogs, just as it is in humans. Unlike humans, however, dogs don't do well with wearing glasses. Have your dog's vision checked at least once a year and more often if it is obvious that his or her eyesight is failing. Those eyes will need extra attention.

- Kidney disease is a common problem in older dogs, and one that you should monitor for the older your Pom gets. If your canine is drinking more often and having accidents regularly, this could be a sign of something more serious than just aging. If you notice this happening, get your Pom to the vet as soon as possible and have him or her checked for kidney disease.

Enjoying The Final Years

The last years of your Pom's life can actually be just as enjoyable (if not more so) than the earlier stages. The energy and activities that the two of you used to do will be replaced with more attention and relaxation than at any other time. Finally having your Pom be calm enough to just sit still and enjoy your company can be incredibly nice (just remember to keep up his or her activity levels instead of getting too complacent with your Pom's new-found love of resting and relaxing).

Steps And Ramps

Poms are small, but that does not mean that you should be picking them up more often as they age. Picking up your dog more often can even do even more physical harm. There are two good reasons to ensure your Pom is able to move around without you picking him or her up.

- Having an older body means they are fragile and should not be picked up to avoid unnecessary pain.
- Independence in movement is best for you and your Pomeranian. You do not want your Pom to come to expect you to pick him or her up every time he or she wants to get on the furniture or into the car.

Steps and ramps are the best way to ensure your Pom can keep some level of self-sufficiency. Also, you don't want to spoil your Pom in the later years. Using steps and ramps provides a bit of different activity that can work as a way of getting a bit of extra exercise.

Enjoy The Advantages

A Pom can be just as much fun in old age because his or her favorite thing is being with you. Your pet is just as mischievous as during the early years, but has learned to chill a bit more.

Your pet will find the warmest and most comfortable places, and will want you to join him or her. Your dog is incredibly devoted and will be happy to just share a short stroll followed by a lazy evening at home.

What To Expect

Your Pomeranian probably isn't going to suffer from fear that you are less interested in spending time together. He or she will continue be the loving mischief maker at every opportunity – that does not change with age. Just how much they can do changes. Your canine's limitations should dictate interactions and activities. If you are busy, make sure you schedule time

CHAPTER 17   Your Aging Pomeranian

with your Pom to do things that are within those limitations. Your happiness is still of utmost importance to your dog, so let the little canine know you feel the same way about his or her happiness. It is just as easy to make an older Pomeranian happy as it is with a young one, and it is easier on you since relaxing is more essential to your old friend.

Vet Visits

As your Pom ages, you are going to notice the slow-down, and the pains in your Pom's body are going to be obvious just like in an older person. You need to make sure that you have regular visits with your vet to make sure that you aren't doing anything that could potentially harm your Pom. If your Pomeranian has a debilitating ailment or condition, you may want to discuss the options for ensuring a better quality of life, such as wheels if your Pom's legs begin to have serious issues. In the worst cases, you may want to discuss the quality of your Pomeranian's life with the vet.

Photo Courtesy of Katrina Campbell

www.ingramcontent.com/pod-product-compliance
Lightning Source LLC
Chambersburg PA
CBHW062053280426
43661CB00087B/648